Where They Lived in London - Vol I

The Lives & Locations of the

Rich, Famous & Interesting

Author: John Pullen

First Edition: 2016

First EBook Edition: 2016

Printed by CreateSpace, An Amazon.com Company

Cover Image Design: JPP

Available from Amazon, CreateSpace.com and other retail outlets

www.johnpullenwriter.com

For

Laure – the perfect chapter

Contents

Michael Faraday

Isaac Newton

Alan Turing

Part One
Actors

Richard Burton

Address: 6 Lyndhurst Road, London NW3

Station: Hampstead Tube

Richard Burton is probably remembered for three things – his presence as a very accomplished actor, his unmistakable voice and the fact that he was married to Elizabeth Taylor twice. He rose to the very top of his career as an A-list actor but his roots were much more ordinary. He was born – Richard Walter Jenkins - on the 10th November 1925 in the South Wales valley village of Pontrhydyfen. Burton would not be short of siblings as he was the twelfth of thirteen. Unfortunately at the age of two he lost his mother to puerperal fever – she was just forty four years of age.

An older sister – Cecilia or Cis as she was known – took him to live in Port Talbot with her and her husband Elfed and two daughters. It was said that he remained grateful for their support throughout his life. But it was his older brother Ifor that he looked up to – in Richard's view Ifor could do anything and when he became successful, invited Ifor to become his personal assistant.

Burton would always have a reputation for wild parties, drinking and chasing women. And he showed promise in each of these areas when he was still a young teenager. He got himself a job in a clothes shop which he hated. Eventually he joined a local youth club and discovered what would become the central driving force in his life – acting. He landed a couple of small parts and they had the effect of getting him back to school to finish his studies.

He met a teacher there – Philip Burton – who took him under his wing. And it was after him that Richard changed his surname from Jenkins to Burton. He now had his stage name. It was also down to Philip that Richard perfected his distinctive speaking voice. It is said that Philip would take him up a mountain and ask him to recite passages whilst he walked further away. Rather than shout to be heard, Richard was told to project himself. And so the famous Richard Burton voice was born.

Richard's studies paid off and he went up to Oxford to further his education. It was here he discovered Shakespeare and his performances in different productions soon earned him praise from high quarters. The New Statesman said he showed "exceptional ability" and some of the "greats" such as John Gielgud and Terrence Rattigan were much impressed.

In the post war years, Burton's reputation continued to grow and many in the business began to predict great things for him. They would not be wrong. Even Hollywood was beginning to take notice. For somebody who lived close to the poverty line for many years, he was now offered a seven picture deal worth $1,000,000. However at the time he was also booked to do a run in the Old Vic at £45 per week. There wasn't any choice for someone who loved words and his profession so much – he chose to stay at the Old Vic.

Burton lived in Hampstead for seven years

In 1949 he married Sybil Williams and they had two daughters – Kate and Jessica. They lived in Hampstead before moving to the Swiss town of Celigny. The marriage ended in divorce in 1963. Perhaps the pivotal point in both his professional and personal life occurred when he was offered the part of Mark Anthony in the film Cleopatra. The title role was to be played by a young Elizabeth Taylor. It was the most expensive film to date and the studio wanted as much publicity as possible.

However they also got a large slice of what they regarded as the wrong sort – Taylor and Burton began an off-screen affair. At the time they were both married. The publicity and gossip machine went into overdrive – the Vatican had something to say about it and there was even a move by the American Congress to ban both of them from entering the USA. However, the studio soon realised that their affair was attracting the interest of a large section of the world and that also meant a bigger interest in their movies.

Burton's house in Hampstead

Their next film – The VIPs – was also a success. Of course, such publicity meant that their marriages would not survive and both sought out divorces. Once together, they became the number one celebrity couple – everyone wanted a piece of them and their careers went from strength to strength. Richard especially became the high living superstar with all the disadvantages of such a lifestyle. He had smoked since the age of eight and he was now on 100 a day. It was only matched by his heavy drinking.

In 1970 he was awarded a CBE by Queen Elizabeth II and he took Cis with him to Buckingham Palace. But his drinking would get worse, especially when Ifor died in 1972. It has been said that this was the trigger for Taylor and Burton to divorce in 1974. Taylor never lost hope in him and they remarried a year later. However, Richard was not comfortable and he met Susan the widow of British racing driver James Hunt. Richard divorced Taylor for a second time and married Susan Hunt. Their marriage lasted until 1982 when they too were divorced. He then met a production assistant on the set of a film he was making. He fell in love with her and they married in 1983. It was to be his last marriage.

His life of living in the fast lane was catching up with him – the smoking and the drinking had almost certainly weakened him and on the 5th August 1984, he died of a cerebral haemorrhage whilst visiting Geneva. He was buried in Celigny with a book of the Collected Poems of Dylan Thomas.

Noel Coward

Address: 17 Gerald Road, London SW1

Station: Victoria Tube

Noel Coward was a man of many talents. By the end of his life he was an accomplished playwright, actor, director, music composer, singer and all-round bon viveur. He was born on the 16th December 1899 in Teddington in south west London. His father was a piano salesman but it would be his mother who was to influence and some might say, push him into the creative arts. She sent him, as a child, to a dance academy in London and encouraged him to go up for auditions for various stage productions.

He was just eleven years old when he won his first professional part in a play. He played Prince Mussel in the children's play The Goldfish. It appears that even at this young age he was confident in his own abilities as evidenced in this excerpt from his first volume of memoirs.

"One day ... a little advertisement appeared in the Daily Mirror.... It stated that a talented boy of attractive appearance was required by a Miss Lila Field to appear in her production of an all-children fairy play: The Goldfish. This seemed to dispose of all argument. I was a talented boy, God knows, and, when washed and smarmed down a bit, passably attractive. There appeared to be no earthly reason why Miss Lila Field shouldn't jump at me, and we both believed that she would be a fool indeed to miss such a magnificent opportunity."

Other appearances followed and he was soon moving within London high society. This seemed to suit him well as his stage work over the coming years would mainly be associated with such circles. He would publish more than 50 plays in his lifetime and many of them live on today such as Blythe Spirit, Present Laughter and Private Lives.

Theatrical musicals were also something he produced in abundance with over twelve to his name.

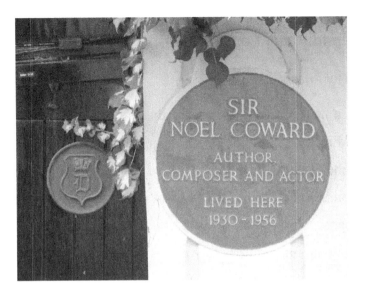

Coward was a multi-talented creative

On the literary side he wrote poetry as well many volumes of short stories. His memoirs which were mentioned earlier covered three volumes. The film industry was not ignored – Coward wrote a number of screenplays as well as having an active acting career. Some of his earlier films have become iconic including the wartime movie In Which We Serve. He won a Honourary Academy Award for his part in the film. His last movie - during which his health was failing – was the first version of The Italian Job starring alongside Michael Caine.

As stated earlier he also wrote many songs and during the 1950s and 60s, he would often perform his own works on stage and couple them with sophisticated humour and observances. He received official public honour in 1969 when he was made a Knight of the Realm by the Queen. In the same year he was elected a Fellow of the Royal Society of Literature and in 2006 he received more recognition when the Albery Theatre was renamed the Noel Coward Theatre.

He spent the years between 1930 and 1956 living at 17 Gerald Road in London. His private life was private although it was openly known that he was gay. But in those days it was not really talked about and Coward preferred it that way. For many years Coward suffered from arteriosclerosis coupled with periods of memory loss. It would be this latter condition which prompted him to give up acting after The Italian Job. He owned an estate in Jamaica – the Firefly Estate – and it was here that he died on the 26th March 1973 of heart failure. He is buried on the island.

Noel Coward's home for 26 years

Boris Karloff

Address: 36 Forest Hill Road, London SE22

Station: Honor Oak Overground

Some actors are typecast for certain roles whilst others are remembered for one part in their career. And there are some who seem to have been born to play one part – and in Boris Karloff's case it was to be Frankenstein's Monster. No other actor is remembered so fondly or in horror at playing this role.

Karloff's house is now a fish & chip shop

He was born William Henry Pratt on the 23rd November 1887 at 36 Forest Hill Road, Camberwell, south London – it is now a shop selling fish and chips. He was the youngest of nine children and when his mother died, he was brought up by his siblings. The family moved to Enfield in Middlesex about ten miles to the north of London where the young boy attended the local grammar school before moving on to private education. He went to King's College London where it was thought he would eventually enter the Consular

Service of the British Government. But it was not to be and he dropped out before taking his final exams.

In 1909 he moved to Canada and took some manual jobs in order to earn money. It was here that he began to dabble in acting and then changed his name to Boris Karloff – he chose Boris because he thought it to be foreign and exotic and Karloff because it was an old Slavic name connected to his family. However it is interesting to note that he never officially changed his name by deed pole. And this was noticeable when it came to him signing autographs – he would write "William H Pratt a.k.a. Boris Karloff."

During his time in Canada he would take parts in plays and then subsidise his meagre earnings with more manual work. This had the effect over time of giving him back problems which would remain with him throughout his life. The effect of his back injury meant that he was not allowed to fight during the First World War. He also had a stutter and a lisp - he was able to cure his stutter but the lisp stayed with him.

At the end of the war he moved to Hollywood and began to pick up small parts in films and other productions. His first official on-screen appearance was in a movie serial called The Masked Rider made in 1919. During the 1920s he still had to do manual work to earn more money but his big break was about to arrive. In 1931 he made three films which would have a significant effect on his career. The first was The Criminal Code from which he received praise for his part. This was followed by Five Star Final in which he played the part of an unethical journalist. The film was nominated for Best Picture. Finally he got the part which many would say was made for him – Frankenstein. With his makeup on and wearing the classic "monster" costume, he became the image of Frankenstein from that moment on. It is said that his shoes had four inch platforms built into them and weighed five kilogrammes each. He certainly did suffer for his art.

Other follow-ups along the Frankenstein theme came his way. But in addition he landed other roles as well including one in the original Scarface and John Ford's iconic film The

Lost Patrol. But he couldn't escape the horror movie image that he had made his own. He starred in such horror genre films as The Mummy, The Raven, The Body Snatcher and The Face of Fu Manchu.

During his career he also made a number of radio shows and often appeared on the stage. His repertoire was not consigned to horror either as he could also play comedy and straight roles just as easily. Karloff had a long and varied career which wasn't helped by his medical problems. Towards the end of his career he developed emphysema which meant that he needed to breath in oxygen from a tank in between takes on set. The last four films he made were for a low budget series of Mexican horror movies.

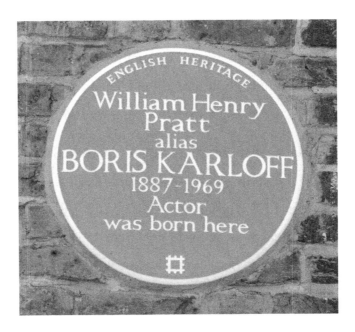

The iconic Frankenstein of movies

He was married five times – his wives were Grace Harding, Montana Laurena Williams, Helene Vivian Soule, Dorothy Stine and Evelyn Hope Helmore who was with him when he died. He had one daughter – Sarah – who born in 1938. He retired from the movie industry and moved back to Britain. He had a house in the village of Bramshott in Hampshire. Whilst there he contracted pneumonia and was taken into hospital. He didn't recover and died on the 2nd February 1969 at the age of 81. There is a memorial plaque to him in the Actors' Church in London's Covent Garden.

Charles Laughton

Address: 15 Percy Street, London W1

Station: Tottenham Court Road Tube

Charles Laughton was another actor who was also a successful scriptwriter, producer and director. As a character actor he was happy on the stage as well as on the screen. He was British being born in the north east of England – Scarborough on the Yorkshire coast – on the 1st July 1899. His parents looked after a hotel in the area. Amongst other places he was educated at Stonyhurst College – one of the best Catholic schools in the country.

He saw action during the First World War serving with the Huntingdonshire Cyclist Battalion. Whilst with them he suffered one of the worst aspects of this war – he was gassed by the enemy. He survived and later transferred to the Northamptonshire Regiment.

15 Percy Street today

After the war he went back to Scarborough to help out in the family hotel. But whilst there, he became interested in the theatre and landed parts in some local productions. It was in 1925 that his theatrical career took a turn for the better – he was accepted to study at one of the foremost acting schools in the country – The Royal Academy of Dramatic Art, known as RADA, in London.

Less than a year later he made his first professional appearance in Barnes Theatre as Osip in the comedy The Government Inspector. By 1928 he was living at 15 Percy Street in London W1 and starring in Sean O'Casey's play The Silver Tassie. He married the actress Elsa Lanchester in 1929 – they stayed together until his death in 1962. When he started his film work in Britain he took some small parts acting opposite his wife who had the lead role. These were silent comedies.

Commemorating Charles Laughton

Laughton moved to the New York stage for the first time and he was soon noticed and offered parts in some Hollywood films. In fact his first such movie – The Old Dark House – included in the cast one Boris Karloff. He was soon playing opposite some of the big stars of the time including Gary Cooper and Cary Grant. In 1933 he played King Henry

VIII in Alexander Korda's production of The Private Life of Henry VIII. It was to be a turning point as he won an Academy Award for his efforts.

Laughton continued to impress and had leading roles such as Captain Bligh in Mutiny on the Bounty with Clark Gable playing Fletcher Christian. The line-up of actors he played opposite with was the "A" List of the Hollywood of the time – Merle Oberon, Vivien Leigh, Rex Harrison, Maureen O'Hara and Robert Newton. But perhaps one of the roles he will be most remembered for is that of Quasimodo in The Hunchback of Notre Dame.

Laughton was also a director and in 1955 he directed The Night of the Hunter starring Robert Mitchum, Shelly Winters and Lillian Gish. Although it was not hailed as a hit at the time of its release, it has since been cited as a film which should be preserved for posterity. To this end, it has been selected by the USA National Film Registry to be kept at the Library of Congress.

Although married to Elsa for thirty three years there were regular stories that Laughton was either gay or bi-sexual. Perhaps he was but his marriage outlasted many other "straight" Hollywood relationships. He lived on a large estate overlooking the Pacific Coast Highway. And it was here that he developed kidney cancer from which he died on the 15th December 1962.

Alastair Sim

Address: 8 Frognal Gardens, London NW3

Station: Hampstead Tube

Alastair Sim was a character actor who was born on the 9th October 1900 in Edinburgh. He worked successfully on both the stage and in film. However, unlike many other actors, he did not begin his theatrical career until he was thirty years of age. This was not to say that he had no involvement in the creative arts. In fact he was a lecturer in elocution at the University of Edinburgh and ran his own drama school. But it was the playwright John Drinkwater who was instrumental in getting him to go forward and tread the boards himself.

Sim lived in Hampstead for twenty two years

He joined the theatrical company at the Old Vic and soon found himself taking parts in a variety of productions including Shakespeare. It was also a time that saw him begin to direct productions for the author James Bridie. By the 1950s he was a leading actor in the

British film industry and would eventually make over fifty movies. And he could turn his hand to comedy as well as drama.

During this period he played in many famous films including the part of Scrooge in A Christmas Carol and the headmistress and her brother in the St Trinian's series of films. In addition he played major roles in Alfred Hitchcock's Stage Fright, The Happiest Days of Your Life, Green for Danger and An Inspector Calls. The 1960s saw Sim go back to the stage where he appeared in such plays as The Tempest, The Merchant of Venice and Peter Pan.

He married Naomi Plaskitt in 1932 and they remained together until his death. They had one daughter – Merlith. Although Sim was a famous actor he shunned the public life which normally follows such success. He never signed autographs and rarely gave interviews. The magazine Focus on Film did manage to get one and Sim delivered a quote about his feelings on the subject of publicity, "I stand or fall in my profession by the public's judgment of my performances. No amount of publicity can dampen a good one or gloss over a bad one."

The imposing family home in Hampstead

During his career he and his wife were enthusiastic about bringing on young acting talent. They would even allow some of the protégés to stay with them at their home near Henley-on-Thames. These young actors included George Cole who remained a friend all his life. In 1953 Sim received a CBE from the Queen. However, when he was offered a knighthood in the 1970s, he refused the honour. He was made Rector to the University of Edinburgh and after this terminated he was awarded a Honourary Doctor of Law from the same university. For part of his life he lived at 8 Frognal Gardens in Hampstead. He was also to die in London. It was due to lung cancer and he passed away on the 19th August 1976. He was aged seventy five.

Part Two

Artists

Canaletto

Address: 41 Beak Street, London W1

Station: Piccadilly Circus Tube

He was born Giovanni Antonio Canal on the 28th October 1697 in Venice. He was the son of another artist – Bernardo Canal. But to everyone he was and is known as Canaletto. This change of name came about quite naturally as it translates as "little Canal". His father specialised in painting theatrical scenery and the young Canaletto followed this genre whilst training with his father and brother. Canaletto is best remembered for his studies of different aspects of life within the city of Venice – its buildings and its inhabitants - and he was influenced in this subject by the Roman artist Giovanni Paolo Pannini.

Plaque marking Canaletto's London home

Canaletto returned to Venice from Rome in 1719 and became acquainted with the work of the artist Luca Carlevarijs. It would not be long before Canaletto began to outperform his master artist and he was urged instead to study the work of Antonio Canale. An aspect of his method of painting was that early on in his career he would complete his work outside. This was unusual as most artists of the time preferred to finish their work from inside their studio. In his later years, Canaletto would also adopt this procedure.

Today it is considered that his earlier work was his best and one in particular – The Stonemason's Yard – is thought by many to be his highlight. On a personal note, I prefer some of his studies of the Grand Canal. All of these paintings are on view at the National Gallery in London.

And speaking of London, Canaletto spent nine years here. But his association with England goes a lot deeper than that. He found that his paintings were popular with many rich English people taking the Grand Tour of Europe. He was helped in this by a businessman and merchant – Joseph Smith – who acted as his agent and salesman. Smith would later become the British Consul to Venice. This association continued from the 1720s to the 1740s until it was brought almost to a halt by the breakout of the War of the Austrian Succession. This had the effect of vastly reducing the number of visitors and his customers to Venice.

The British market must have been very important to Canaletto because in 1746 he moved to London in order to be close to where he could sell his works. However it also meant that he could now diversify his subject matter and he began to paint views of London and the surrounding districts. In addition he received commissions from rich patrons who requested him to create paintings of their homes and estates. Being such a popular artist he was able to flourish and he also produced paintings of Westminster Bridge as well as Westminster Abbey close by.

Now it has been suggested that whilst in England many of his patrons asked him to address their subject matter in the same style as they were used to seeing in his earlier works of Venice. This had the effect of stifling his creativity and it could be seen in his work. It was as if he were painting by formula. In fact at one time, things got so bad that he was accused of employing an imposter to paint his work. To set the record straight

Canaletto felt compelled to paint in public in order to prove that he was still the original artist producing these works.

Canaletto's house in Beak Street, Soho

Unfortunately although he "won his case" it is felt that his reputation never returned to the heady days of his earlier works. In 1755 Canaletto moved back to Venice. Eight years later he was elected to the Venetian Academy and after that, installed as prior to the Collegio dei Pittori. He died at the age of 70 in Venice on the 19th April 1768.

John Constable

Address: 40 Well Walk, London NW3

Station: Hampstead Tube

John Constable was an English artist of the nineteenth century who many believe was the equal of Turner. Indeed they would be competitors for many years of their professional lives'. Constable was born in the Suffolk village of East Bergholt on the 11th June 1776. The village and the surrounding district would be the subjects of some of his greatest paintings. The area today is fondly known as "Constable Country".

He was once asked by his friend John Fisher in 1821 why he chose some of his subjects so close to home. He answered that it was all about feeling, "I should paint my own places best…painting is but another word for feeling."

From an early age Constable would walk around the area with his sketchbook – he would later say that he loved and was inspired by what he saw and heard. However, it would be an art collector by the name of George Beaumont who would trigger his desire to be a great artist. Beaumont had within his collection a painting by the renowned artist Claude Lorrain. It was titled Hagar and the Angel. Constable was much taken by it. Now Constable's father was a wealthy corn merchant and the young Constable was urged to work in the family business. This he did but the lure of being a full-time professional artist grew stronger within him.

In 1799 he won his case and his father gave him permission to make art his profession. He even provided a small but steady income so that he would not starve before becoming successful. The first thing he did was enter the Royal Academy School in London where he attended many classes in art and other complimentary subjects. He became much influenced by other great painters such as Gainsborough and Peter Paul Rubens. Constable must have been a good student for by 1803 he was exhibiting some of his work at the Royal Academy.

Constable would become a great landscape artist and in 1802 he wrote a letter to the master of the Royal Academy – Benjamin West – outlining where his professional interest lay. "For the last two years I have been running after pictures, and seeking the truth at second hand... I have not endeavoured to represent nature with the same elevation of mind with which I set out, but have rather tried to make my performances look like the work of other men...There is room enough for a natural painter. The great vice of the present day is bravura, an attempt to do something beyond the truth."

Plaque outside Constable's Hampstead home

This was a time where romantic views of landscapes were becoming popular and Constable had not yet adopted this style. So to make some extra money he painted portraits for rich patrons. But his heart was not in such subjects. The likely trigger to finding the subject and style that would mark him out amongst other artists was when he visited his friend John Fisher who lived with his family in the city of Salisbury. The spectacular cathedral of Salisbury and the countryside around truly inspired him and fired his imagination. Paintings of Salisbury Cathedral, Dedham Vale, Boat-Building at Flatford Mill, The Cornfield and The Hay Wain amongst many others would become some of the best loved pictures of all time.

The love of his life was Maria Bicknell whom he had known since childhood. Unfortunately any marriage was opposed by her family because they considered Constable to be too poor to support her adequately. Even his own parents agreed with this summary of his position.

However things would change when both his father and mother died within a short time of each other and he inherited one fifth of the estate. John and Maria were eventually married at St Martin-in-the-Field church in Trafalgar Square, London in October 1816.

Constable often refused to travel in order to promote and sell his work. In fact it is believed he only sold about twenty paintings in his home country during his lifetime. But his work was better received in France where it is noted that he sold approximately the same number there in only a few years.

Tragedy was about to strike which would change both him and his style of work. After giving birth to their seventh child, Maria fell ill with tuberculosis and died on the 23rd November 1828 – she was only 41 years of age. Constable was devastated at her loss. He brought up his children without help and he changed his appearance by usually dressing in black. He speculated by producing engravings of some of his works but they were not a financial success.

However, on the positive side he was elected a member of the Royal Academy in February 1829. He also began to give public lectures on landscape painting which were well received. He spoke of a three-fold thesis on the subject – first that landscape painting is scientific as well as poetic. Secondly, that imagination always comes second to the reality of the subject and lastly, that no great artist was ever self-taught.

Constable lived in Hampstead in north London and it was here that he died of suspected heart failure on the 31st March 1837. He is buried with his beloved Maria locally in the churchyard of St John-at-Hampstead.

Constable's London home

Dante Gabriel Rossetti

Address: 110 Hallam Street, London W1

Station: Great Portland Street Tube

Dante Gabriel Rossetti was not only a painter of great regard but also a poet and illustrator. He was born on the 12th May 1828 at 110 Hallam Street in London. His father was an Italian scholar. Although his friends referred to him as Gabriel, he preferred Dante which was after Dante Alighieri – the author of Dante's Inferno. Both of his sisters and his brother became known for their creative talents in writing, critique and poetry.

Rossetti preferred Dante to his real name of Gabriel

The young Dante attended King's College School before enrolling at the Antique School of the Royal Academy. He showed an early interest in Medieval Italian Art. During his life Dante would make friends and associations with some of the finest artists and creatives of the time including Ford Maddox-Brown, William Holman-Hunt and John

Everett Millais. It would be with the latter two that he set up the Pre-Raphaelite Brotherhood.

Their philosophy was to change British art from a more formal rigid approach espoused by artists such as Sir Joshua Reynolds. In their eyes, compositions were to become more detailed and employing intense colour in their works. They were in fact basing this method on ones in use within the Italian and Flemish art world. Perhaps their philosophy was best summed up by the critic John Ruskin who wrote, "Every Pre-Raphaelite landscape background is painted to the last touch, in the open air, from the thing itself. Every Pre-Raphaelite figure, however studied in expression, is a true portrait of some living person."

House where Rossetti was born

In 1849 Rossetti exhibited his first major work – The Girlhood of Mary Virgin. It was well received and earned critical praise for his method of painting. William Bell Scott witnessed his technique and wrote, "He was painting in oils with water colour brushes, as thinly as in water colour, on canvas which he had primed with white till the surface was as smooth as cardboard, and every tint remained transparent. I saw at once that he was not an orthodox boy, but acting purely from the aesthetic motive. The mixture of genius and dilettantism of both men shut me up for the moment, and whetted my curiosity."

Unfortunately his next major work entitled Ecce Ancilla Domini did not go well with the critics. They were turning against the Pre-Raphaelite style and Rossetti felt so injured by the criticism that he dropped oil painting and turned to water colours for a while. These he sold privately preferring not to exhibit his work for fear of further criticism. Rossetti would rarely publicly exhibit his work again in his lifetime.

This happened in 1850 but the year was not all bad for him. He also met his future bride the same year. Her name was Elizabeth Siddal. It would be another ten years before they married in 1860. During these years she became one of the main models for all the artists of the Pre-Raphaelite movement. But she became much more to Rossetti – first as a model, then a pupil and finally, his wife.

Much of his inspiration came from the romantic tales of Arthurian legend. Not only would he use their stories as a basis of his works but he also translated Italian poetry from his hero Dante Alighieri. In future years Rossetti's work would influence others such as William Morris and Edward Burne-Jones.

In 1862, Elizabeth died of an overdose of laudanum taken after she gave birth to a still-born child. Rossetti was devastated at her loss. To keep her memory alive Rossetti painted her image in a number of paintings including Beata Beatrix. Although depressed he still had a lover who also posed as a model for him. Her name was Fanny Cornforth.

Rossetti now moved to 16 Cheyne Walk in Chelsea. Fanny did not live with him but was "kept" in a house conveniently near to him. He was to spend twenty years at this address. Besides his interests in legend and poetry he also developed an intense interest in exotic animals and especially in wombats. He owned a couple of the creatures and allowed them the run of the house including access to the dinner table when he was entertaining guests.

In addition, when asked to meet someone, he would often suggest the wombat house at the London Zoo as the location. Later on in his life he would also purchase a toucan and a llama – both of which shared the house in Cheyne Walk. It is reported that he would sometimes dress the llama up in a cowboy hat and ride it on top of the dining table for the "entertainment" of his guests. One might begin to question where his mind was going at this stage of his life.

His condition did come to a head in 1872 after he received bad reviews for a collection of poetry he had published. He had a nervous breakdown which took a year to recover from. Unfortunately during this period he began to rely on alcohol and drugs to keep himself going. Over the coming years they were to take a stronger hold over him and he became an addict. It is said that close to the end he would drink large amounts of whisky in order to take away the bad taste of the drugs he was taking.

He died on the 9th April 1882 aged just 53 years. But his work is held in high esteem and his art and poetry has been responsible for influencing many people since including Claude Debussy, Ralph Vaughn Williams and John Ireland amongst many others.

JMW Turner

Address: 119 Cheyne Walk, London SW3

Station: Sloane Square Tube

Joseph Mallord William Turner was born in Maiden Lane Covent Garden around April 1775. Turner would always claim it was on the 23rd but we have no evidence for this. But what we can be sure of was that he was baptised on the 14th May. His father was a barber and his mother came from a family of butchers. He had a sister but she died as a child.

Turner was a controversial figure during his lifetime but most people today would regard him as perhaps the greatest landscape artist this country has produced. His use of light took both his oil paintings and his watercolours to new heights. In fact he was known as "the painter of light".

When he was ten, his mother was admitted to hospital suffering from mental problems. Turner was first sent to an uncle in Brentford in west London and then a year later, to Margate on the Kent coast. It was during these periods that we have the first sketches made by the future artist. Soon his "pictures" were being sold by his father in his barber shop – Turner was beginning to be paid for his work.

During these periods, Turner developed a style of working which he would keep in later life. It became his method to sketch what he saw on location and then take the sketches back to his studio where he would create the painting. Some of his sketchbooks are still in existence and can be viewed at galleries such as Tate Britain in London.

At fourteen Turner enrolled at the Royal Academy School. Only a year later, he was admitted to the Royal Academy itself. The president who sat on the committee that allowed him entry was none other than Sir Joshua Reynolds. Turner's first watercolour was accepted to be exhibited in the Royal Academy Summer Exhibition when he was still only fifteen years old. It would be a bone of contention that Tuner would say that John Constable – his artistic rival – was fifty three before he was admitted to the Academy.

Over the coming years Turner toured Great Britain to make his sketches which he would later turn into watercolours in the studio. He particularly liked the landscapes of Wales. It was in 1796 that he exhibited – again at the Royal Academy – his first oil painting. It featured The Needles on the west tip of the Isle of Wight bathed in moonlight. He was able to contrast the cold light of the moon with the warm fire glow from a fisherman's lantern. The seascape would be one of Tuner's main themes throughout his life. His next ventures took him overseas and in 1802 he travelled to France and Switzerland. Other trips would take him to Italy and in particular Venice. He also found time to study at The Louvre in Paris.

Turner lived and died at 119 Cheyne Walk

It has been said that Turner could be a difficult fellow and indeed it does appear that as he grew older, his behaviour became more erratic. He had few close friends. His father was an exception and in fact he spent thirty years living with him. It was also a professional relationship as his father became his studio assistant for much of this time. When his father died in 1829 it had a deep and long-lasting effect on Turner. He began to suffer further periods of depression.

Turner never married but he did have two relationships that we know of. They both involved widows. The first was with Sarah Danby and it is said that she bore him two daughters. His other relationship was more open in a strange sort of way. Her name was Sophia Caroline Booth and they lived together in Cheyne Walk for eighteen years. However, because they were not married, society was likely to frown upon them. So Turner adopted the name of Mr Booth in order to attempt to quell any criticism.

Decorative plaque outside 119 Cheyne Walk

Turner died at 119 Cheyne Walk, Chelsea on the 19th December 1851. He is buried in St Paul's Cathedral next to Sir Joshua Reynolds. He left his collection of finished paintings to the nation. Although initially it was difficult to find a fitting and permanent home for the collection, it is now all available for anyone to see at the Clore Gallery within Tate Britain in London. As a further point, perhaps his best loved painting of The Fighting Temeraire is housed at The National Gallery in Trafalgar Square.

Vincent Van Gough

Address: 87 Hackford Road, London SW9

Station: Stockwell Tube

Vincent Van Gogh is probably one of the best known and loved artists in the world today. His works can be seen at many of the foremost galleries. But during his lifetime he did not make much money from his paintings and was very much neglected by the public as an artist of great talent.

He was born on the 30th March 1853 at Groot-Zundert in the southern Netherlands. His father was a minister in the Dutch Reformed Church and as such, had a middle-class upbringing. He was not a well child and suffered a number of bouts of illness. He didn't paint in his youth but did complete some sketches. In fact it would not be until he was in his late 20s that he took up painting. And if we consider he died young, most of the works we have come to love were all completed in the last few years of his life. It was an amazing achievement in such a short time.

Van Gogh was an intellectual and would think deeply about things. He also held strong religious beliefs – no doubt due to the influence of his father. When he was in his 20s he joined a firm of art dealers and found himself spending time working in The Hague, London and Paris. His work is known for its broad brushstrokes and vivid colours but his first major painting – The Potato Eaters – which was produced in the mid-1880s, was none of these things. It was instead a study using dark earthy tones of colour. His real style was yet to be discovered.

This change perhaps began in 1886 when he moved to Paris and became aware of the French Impressionist School. This was further enhanced when he moved to the south of France and was influenced by the bright sunlight and colours of the landscape. His own particular style began to grow and proliferate. He moved to Arles and it is believed that in the next ten years he produced over 2,100 artworks including 860 oil paintings. This is a staggering output.

But already his health was suffering and one of the contributory reasons was his lifestyle. In simple terms he smoked and drank too much. During this time he had visits from other artists. One of these was Paul Gauguin. Van Gogh at this time was living in The Yellow House and he was quite excited by the prospect of Gauguin's visit as he hoped that his dream of starting an artists' collective or colony would become a reality. To this end he bought new beds and furniture. Up until now, Van Gogh had produced paintings of the surrounding countryside but now he painted subjects within the house. These included Van Gogh's Chair and Gauguin's Chair.

Van Gough lived in London for one year

When Gauguin arrived they began painting together. Unfortunately they were of very different characters. Van Gogh desperately wanted to be recognised by Gauguin as his equal but Gauguin was a person with an arrogant and domineering personality. They began to row and fall out with each other. This was to culminate in the famous event of the cutting off of Van Gogh's ear. Accounts of what exactly happened vary depending on whether you believe Van Gogh or Gauguin.

However, objective evidence leads many to believe that Van Gogh at the time was suffering from psychosis and that in one particular episode he took a razor to his left ear and severed it. Some think that it was in reaction to his belief that Gauguin had had enough and was about to leave their home. What happened next is even stranger and lends further evidence that Van Gogh was suffering a breakdown. He is said to have bandaged his ear up although the blood loss was large and then wrapped up the severed ear in a paper package. He is then thought to have delivered the package to a friend of his – Rachael – who worked at a local brothel much frequented by him and Gauguin.

Luckily for Van Gogh he was found the next day by the police - collapsed through blood loss. They took him to a nearby hospital where he was treated. However the police ordered the hospital to detain Van Gogh against his will because of his mental state. He was released home in January of the next year but it was plain that he still had serious problems. Eventually he agreed to be detained at an asylum in Saint-Remy-de-Provence on the 8th May 1889. Over the year he was to spend there, he used the hospital's gardens for his artistic studies.

When he was discharged from the hospital in 1890 he was still not well. For a while he continued to draw and paint but the end was not far in coming. On the 27th July 1890 Van Gogh was either in a wheat field which he had recently painted or in a barn close by. There was a shot from a revolver and Van Gogh received a serious chest wound. It was apparently a suicide attempt although the gun has never been recovered and there were no witnesses to the incident.

However, Van Gogh was able to make his way back to the village where he was attended to by two local doctors. There didn't appear to be any damage to any of the major organs but the bullet still remained in the body. Neither of the attending doctors was skilled in surgery and so they patched him up as best as they could and left him in bed at home smoking his pipe. He seemed to be relatively well considering. The night passed and the next morning his brother Theo arrived after being told of what had happened. He found Van Gogh in good sorts.

But this was not to remain the case. Later in the day he began to decline. The doctors believed that although the major organs had escaped injury he may well have contracted an infection from the wound. The end came quickly and he died that evening aged just thirty seven years. According to his brother who was present, his last words were, "The sadness will last forever."

Van Gogh obviously suffered from psychological problems for a large part of his life and over the years many specialists have tried to pin down the exact conditions he may have suffered from. These have ranged from epilepsy, bipolar disease to schizophrenia to name but three. At the end of the day we just don't know but we can surmise that his lifestyle of overwork, insomnia, undereating and over drinking did not help.

The house is in need of some repair

But before we leave him, let's take a look back to a link we have of him to London. On the 19th May 1873 Van Gogh arrived in London to work for the art dealers Goupil & Co who were located in Southampton Street. And from August 1873 we know that his address in London was 87 Hackford Road just south of the Oval in south London. The road in fact was the subject of one of the sketches he made whilst living there. Today the area around the property has been designated a conservation area. However, the house itself does appear to need some work applied to it.

Part Three

Composers & Musicians

Edward Elgar

Address: 42 Netherhall Gardens, London NW3

Station: Hampstead Tube

You only have to listen to the Last Night of the Proms to understand the effect Edward Elgar had on British and in particular English music. It is hard not to be stirred by Land of Hope and Glory – part of his Pomp and Circumstance Marches. But amazingly, Elgar's musical knowledge came mainly from self-teaching.

He was born in the West Midlands in the village of Broadheath on the 2nd June 1857. The young Elgar did have one advantage from an early age – his father owned a music shop in nearby Worcester. And it was there that Elgar fist studied music and learned to play a variety of instruments that were on hand.

As a young adult he taught the violin and composed and played music for a number of local organisations. Being a Catholic one of his regular responsibilities was to play the organ at St George's Church in Worcester. On the negative side, he was to find some opposition to his works by some members of the Church of England who were of course Protestants.

However, his teaching duties did lead to one big bonus - he met and later married one of his pupils. Her name was Caroline Alice Roberts. But similar to John Constable earlier in this book, her family were not in favour of the marriage because being the daughter of a deceased Major-General and Knight of the Realm they felt that he was beneath her. Luckily for them both, love won out and they were married in 1889. It was to be a good match and they remained together until her death.

Elgar began composing some of his major works in the 1890s including in 1899, his Variations on an Original Theme which became better known as the Enigma Variations. It was a piece that marked Elgar as a force and one of the leading composers in the country. It was followed by one of his greatest religious works – The Dream of Gerontius – based on a poem by Cardinal Newman. Unfortunately its premiere performance had not been rehearsed sufficiently and the reviews were not complimentary. This affected Elgar for a few days but because he was of a determined character, he quickly put it to the back of his mind and began to write further pieces.

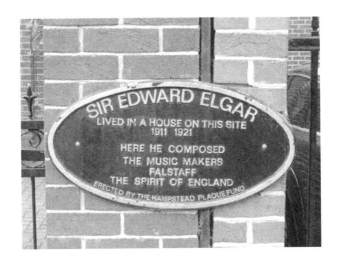

Elgar lived here when his wife died

Incidentally, about a year later, the composition was performed again – this time in Germany. It went well and six months later a third performance was put on – again in Germany. One of those present was Richard Strauss who commented afterwards that Edward Elgar was now the "first English progressive musician."

In 1902 Elgar composed his Pomp and Circumstance Marches. From these a section would become known as Land of Hope and Glory. It is one of his best known and best loved pieces. From the start Elgar himself knew he had a winner on his hands and he said of it, "I've got a tune that will knock 'em flat – knock 'em flat." He was right.

The new century saw him composing his symphonies beginning with Symphony No 1 in A flat which received its first public performance in Manchester in December 1908.

Another followed in 1911 – Symphony No 2 in E flat. It was not as popular as the first but it was remarked upon as capturing the country's mourning after the death of the King – Edward VII.

There were two events in Elgar's life which were to change his style of music. The first was the outbreak of World War I in 1914. Like so many other people, the horror and brutality of the conflict depressed him deeply. At the cessation of hostilities in 1918, Elgar wrote three pieces of chamber music. However it was noticed that these did not have the swagger and bravado of some of his earlier works. War it seems was not something to celebrate in any way.

In 1920 Elgar suffered a personal loss – his wife Alice died. For all of their married life she had been not only his rock but she also provided much of his inspiration. And now she was gone. His work virtually dried up and he went back to Worcestershire – the county of his birth – and became a country gentleman in retirement. But he didn't give up work completely – he would sometimes return to London and elsewhere to conduct performances.

A new house now stands on the site

He was also not forgotten by the Establishment – in 1928 he was made a Knight Commander of the Victorian Order. It perhaps helped to trigger a new surge of creativity for he began to write and compose again. He also began to write an opera. But he did not have long to live. In 1933 he went to Paris to conduct his violin concerto which featured a young Yehudi Menuhin. He also took time out to visit his friend and fellow composer Delius at his home in Grez-sur-Loing. Both of them would be dead within a year.

Elgar was to develop a cancerous tumour and he died on the 23rd February 1934.

Jimi Hendrix

Address: 23 Brook Street, London W1

Station: Bond Street Tube

When Jimi Hendrix got hold of his first electric guitar, the sound of that instrument was going to change forever. He introduced a number of innovations that laid open the amazing possibilities that he and it could produce. And he was able to achieve all these things within four years. What's even more staggering is that he couldn't read or write music.

Remembering Hendrix's stay in London

His real name was Johnny Allen Hendrix and he was born on the 27th November 1942 in Seattle in the USA. From a young age he showed a real interest in music and his father was able to help him by buying him a one-stringed ukulele. This might at first appear to be a bad joke but up until then, Jimi had been using a broom to imitate playing a guitar and a lot of imagination.

Jimi's method of understanding music came from listening to the stars of the day on the radio. They included artistes such as Buddy Holly, BB King and Muddy Waters to name a few. It was said that he would concentrate hard on how the music sounded rather than how it was written.

In 1958 the ukulele was replaced by his first guitar. His father paid $5 for it. This seems to have been his springboard into a musical career for a little later, he joined his first band. They called themselves the Velvetones. He lasted three months before he left the band in order to go solo. Things improved for Jimi when, a few months later, his father bought him his first electric guitar. It was a Supro Ozark 1560S. This led to him joining another band called The Rocking Kings.

But his life wasn't all music. In 1961 Jimi joined the US Army and became a paratrooper. Unfortunately for the Army but good for the music industry, Jimi sustained a parachuting injury and was discharged from the service. Back as a civilian again he found work as a session musician backing up many famous artistes. These included Tina Turner, the Isley Brothers and Little Richard. The name he went under now was Jimmy James.

His next move was to form his own band. It was called Jimmy James and the Blue Flames. Jimi promoted himself from session to lead guitarist. It was during this period that he met The Animal's bass guitarist Chas Chandler. He eventually persuaded Jimi to leave America and move to London. The intention was for Jimi to found a new band there. Chas Chandler became his manager and it was he that also changed Jimi's name from Jimmy James to Jimi Hendrix. With Mitch Mitchell on drums and Noel Reddin on bass, The Jimi Hendrix Experience was formed.

Their first single was Hey Joe and it spent ten weeks in the Hit Parade reaching a high of number six in early 1967. It wasn't long before they produced their first album entitled Are You Experienced. It consisted of a compilation of psychedelic anthems such as Purple Haze, Foxey Lady and Fire. The band was now famous but much more was to come. They returned to the USA in June 1967 and played at the Monterey International Pop Festival. Almost overnight they became one of the hottest bands on the planet.

Jimi built his own recording studio so that he could exert even more control over his unique style of music. It was called Electric Lady Studios and was located in New York. Unfortunately the studio work and the touring took their toll and the band disbanded in 1969. But perhaps Jimi's best known performance came at the iconic music festival held in Woodstock in 1969. He joined a collection of other musicians on stage but it was his version of the Star Spangled Banner that sent the crowd into a frenzy.

Hendrix lived here with his girlfriend

In 1969 Jimi returned to London where he performed at the Royal Albert Hall and did a tour of some European countries. During this time he lived at his girlfriend's flat at 23 Brook Street London. Her name was Kathy Etchingham.

In 1970 The Jimi Hendrix Experience reformed but with Billy Cox on bass. He began working on a new project - a double album. However, once again the touring and workload on Jimi was taking its toll. For some years Jimi had drunk too much and taken illegal substances. He died in London on the 18th September 1970. The post-mortem said that he died by suffocating on his own vomit after taking barbiturates. He is buried next to his mother in Renton, Washington.

Gustav Holst

Address: St Paul's Girls' School, Brook Green, London W8

Station: Hammersmith Tube

Ask most people if they can name a piece of music composed by Gustav Holst and it is almost a sure bet that they will say The Planet Suite. It is what he is best remembered for. But there was a lot more to his musical credentials than that. Besides being a composer of individual style, he was also an arranger as well as a renowned music teacher.

He was born on the 21st September 1874 in Cheltenham. Not only was his father – Adolph – a professional musician but there had been a musician in the family for the previous three generations. Gustav's mother – Clara – died in February 1882 and so his aunt was recruited by his father to help raise the family. His father remarried but it is said that his new "mother" was not too interested in the children.

As a child, Gustav was first taught to play the piano and the violin – at the age of twelve he trained on the trombone. Part of the reason for this was to improve Gustav's health – he suffered from asthma. In addition he also had neuritis which weakened his arm so much that any thoughts of becoming a professional pianist were not going to happen. His final medical problem left him with bad eyesight.

He was first educated at Cheltenham Grammar School and then some months at Oxford studying music under George Frederick Sims who was the organist at Merton College. The short time he spent at Oxford did appear to pay dividends as he soon found a position as organist and choirmaster at Wyke Rissington in Gloucestershire. It also meant that he assumed responsibility as the conductor of the Bourton-on-the-Water Choral Society.

In May 1893 Gustav received a place at the Royal College of Music in London. He didn't receive a scholarship and since his father was not rich, Gustav found himself leading an austere lifestyle. It is said that it was this lack of money that made Gustav become a vegetarian and a teetotaller. Later on he did earn a scholarship but it didn't alter his new lifestyle. Two years after entering the Royal College of Music he met another composer who would remain a life-long friend – his name was Ralph Vaughn Williams.

They were not only friends but were each other's chief critics. It seemed to work well and Williams was later to say that, "What one really learns from an Academy or College is not so much from one's official teachers as from one's fellow-students ... every subject under the sun (was discussed) from the lowest note of the double bassoon to the philosophy of Jude the Obscure."

Gustav had produced a number of compositions but after turning down a further year at the RCM he turned to playing the trombone professionally. He had some success, touring with a number of orchestras including the Scottish Orchestra but it still didn't really make him enough money to live on. He has been quoted as saying, "Man cannot live on compositions alone."

Holst taught at this school

On the 22nd January 1901, Gustav married his love Isobel at Fulham Registry Office. They would remain together until Gustav's death. The union bore one child – a daughter

68

Imogen – who was born in 1907. She would eventually write a biography of her father. Gustav suffered a personal tragedy in 1903 when his father died. The only small advantage from this event was that Gustav was left a small amount of money. He and Isobel decided that since they had scrimped for so long, they would spend the money on a holiday in Germany.

To many observers this would be a turning point in Gustav's life. During the holiday he looked carefully at his life and where it was going. On their return Gustav decided that he would give up playing and instead concentrate on composing music. But he also needed a steady income and so he combined it with teaching music. One of the establishments he taught at was St Paul's School for Girls based in Hammersmith west London. He became their Director of Music in 1905 – it was a post he would hold until his death.

His methods of teaching the girls inspired many of them to take up music as a profession or at least as a serious study. In fact two of his pupils would go on to carve out respectable careers in music. One of them – Joan Cross – became a well-known soprano. Another by the name of Helen Gaskell made history by becoming the first woman to join the woodwind section of the New Queen's Hall Orchestra. Subsequently she went on to play with the BBC Symphony Orchestra.

Whilst living and working at St Paul's School, Gustav would produce his most well-known and best-loved composition – The Planets. He originally had the idea in 1913 because of his interest in astrology. It would be another year before he began writing it. The final "planet" Mercury was completed in 1916. Each piece has a very individual character of its own. Mars, the God of War conjures up images of war, violence and terror. Others such as Saturn, the Bringer of Old Age repeats chords which makes one feel that age is relentless in its journey. Jupiter, the Bringer of Joy has been incorporated into a patriotic hymn I Vow to Thee My Country. Gustav was happy with the adaptation but apparently not everyone else was.

Gustav continued to write new compositions whilst teaching. He was never a gregarious person and much preferred to get on with his work quietly rather than endure the trappings of fame which came after The Planets. In 1932 he did a lecture tour of the USA but during his time there he developed a duodenal ulcer. He went into hospital and eventually was released and he returned to England. He spent the next year working but his health was declining.

Holst composed the Planet Suite at St Paul's School for Girls

He was told that a major operation would allow him to live life normally again and it was arranged to go ahead in May 1934. The operation itself was a success but Gustav's heart was put under an enormous strain. He died two days later on the 25th May 1934. His ashes are buried in Chichester Cathedral.

John Lennon

Address: 34 Montagu Square, London W1

Station: Marble Arch Tube

Ask almost anyone to name some of the most influential pop performers of the twentieth century and The Beatles will almost certainly be on the list. But not only that, it is likely that some of the individuals within the group would also be mentioned in their own right. And the name of John Lennon would likely be near or at the top of that list.

Lennon was born on the 9th October 1940 in Liverpool. His father, Alfred was a merchant seaman. Whilst he was in his mid-teens, Lennon formed a band called The Quarrymen. It took its name from a school he had attended – Quarry Bank High School. The line-up was pretty amazing of course consisting of Paul McCartney, George Harrison and eventually Ringo Starr. The name of the band changed to The Beatles and the rest, as they say, is history.

Initially, they played at clubs in and around Liverpool including the legendary Cavern Bar. But they also ventured overseas and played venues in Hamburg in Germany. Their careers really took off in 1963 when they released the single "Love Me Do" and Beatlemania was born. Other successful singles followed including "Please, Please Me." Within a year the massive American market discovered them. They went over to the States and appeared on the top-rated "Ed Sullivan Show." Two years later the Queen presented them all with MBEs. However, being a person of strong human values, Lennon felt compelled to return his award four years later as a protest against war.

The Beatles popularity continued to soar until Lennon made a remark which in hindsight may have been one of the first contributing factors in the group's eventual demise. He remarked that their band was "more popular than Jesus." There were many protests at their gigs and coupled with the stresses of touring around the world, it began to take its toll on the group. They quit touring and instead concentrated on producing work in the studio.

Plaque to Lennon in London

During much of this time Lennon had been married but in the late 1960s he met and married the artist Yoko Ono. This coincided with the break-up of The Beatles. Some say that she was one of the catalysts for the break-up but others give different reasons. Lennon and Yoko began to work together. Their early albums were not successful and have now been looked on as being experimental. But things changed with their release of the album "Live Peace in Toronto."

Lennon's biggest solo hit came in the early 1970s – it was the song "Imagine" and it is still held up as being one of the most iconic songs of all time. Whether it was due to their new success or not, Lennon and Yoko moved to the United States. However, his political views nearly got him deported. He fought a four year court battle and won his case to stay.

This period of conflict also saw John and Yoko split up. It lasted about a year before they became reunited when Lennon was guesting during an Elton John concert in 1974.

Lennon's London home in 1968

The reunion produced a son – Sean Lennon. This seemed to change the dynamics of the couple with Lennon seeming to settle down as a house-husband whilst Yoko took on the mantle of becoming his business manager. After a few years they produced a new album together entitled "Double Fantasy." Things were beginning to go really well for them but tragedy was about to strike.

They had made their home in New York City living in an apartment block on the west side of Central Park called The Dakotas. On the 8th December 1980, Lennon was about to enter the building after a recording session when a lone gunman - Mark Chapman – approached him and fired four bullets into his back. Lennon died soon after. Chapman, a demented ex-Beatles fan had ended the life of not only a very talented composer and musician but also somebody who genuinely wanted to find a way to save the world he loved.

Ralph Vaughn Williams

Address: 10 Hanover Terrace, Regent's Park London NW1

Station: St John's Wood Tube

Ralph Vaughan Williams was a British music composer who was fascinated with English folk songs and music from the Tudor period. He is also acknowledged as the founder of the Nationalist movement in English music.

Regent's Park home of Vaughn Williams

Vaughan Williams was born on the 12th October 1872 in Gloucestershire. His general and musical education was impressive – he graduated from Trinity College, Cambridge and then entered the prestigious Royal College of Music in London. One of his tutors was the composer Sir Hubert Parry who is best remembered for his choral song Jerusalem which is sung at The Last Night of the Proms. This was followed up in 1897 when he moved to Berlin for a year where he studied under the composer Max Bruch.

It was in 1903 that Vaughan Williams began to collect English folk songs. A year later saw him becoming the editor of "The English Hymnal." At the outbreak of World War I, he joined the artillery with whom he served during the whole of the conflict. After the war he moved back to the Royal College of Music – but this time as Professor of Compositions.

His ongoing interest in folk songs and music from the Tudor period began to influence his own compositions and his work covered many areas including orchestral, chamber music and vocal pieces. He also composed a number of symphonies which included a London Symphony, Sinphonia Antarctica and Fantasia on a Theme by Thomas Tallis. His choral works include Mass in G-Minor, the cantata Towards Unknown Regions and the oratorio Sancta Civitas.

Along with other composers such as Parry, Elgar and Stanford, Vaughan Williams was partly responsible for breaking the musical connection with Europe that had existed for about two hundred years. He and they were able to introduce an English or British style of music based on the music of the past. He died in London on the 26th August 1958 but his legacy will be long remembered.

He spent his final years at this address

Part Four

Doctors & Nurses

Edith Cavell

Address: London Hospital, London E1

Station: Whitechapel Tube

Wars by definition split countries, populations and even families. But during such horror and conflict there are a few people who do not differentiate between friend and enemy. They are not conscientious objectors because they take an active part often close to the front line. Who are these people? They are the doctors and nurses who do not see a friend or foe – only those injured who need their help.

Edith Cavell

Edith Cavell was all these things and more. She was a nurse during the First World War who helped to save lives without discrimination. But more than this, she also helped over 200 Allied soldiers to escape from German occupied Belgium. For these acts she eventually paid the ultimate price.

Edith was born on the 4th December 1865 in the village of Swardeston in Norfolk. Her father was a vicar in the Church of England. She was educated at Norwich High School for Girls. After she left school she travelled to Brussels where she became a governess to a family.

When she returned to England Edith decided she wanted to be a nurse and so she enrolled at the London Hospital in Whitechapel. Her connections in Belgium came to the fore again and after she had qualified, she was recruited to work as the matron of a new nursing school in Brussels. It was called The Berkendael Medical Institute under the management of Dr Antoine Depage.

Cavell worked at the London Hospital in Whitechapel

Three years later she was instrumental in publishing a professional journal for nurses entitled L'Infirmiere. By 1911 Edith had become responsible as the training nurse for three hospitals, twenty four schools and thirteen kindergartens in Belgium.

World War I broke out in 1914 and Edith was back in England at the time visiting her mother who was now a widow. She could have stayed in England away from the danger but that was not in her character. Edith returned to Brussels to find that both her clinic and nursing school were now under the control of the Red Cross.

The German troops invaded Belgium and in November 1914 captured Brussels. Any casualties who came into her care – Allied or German – were treated. But she was also taking another active role – a very secretive one – in helping Allied soldiers avoid capture and to reach the safety of neighbouring Holland which was neutral in the war.

The method of getting the soldiers to Holland required a sophisticated network. False papers would be produced for each escapee and they would be kept in one of a number of safe houses in Belgium. This is where Edith came in. She would hide them and then provide money and a local guide to help them reach the Dutch border and freedom.

However the Germans were not stupid and they knew such networks existed. They also suspected Edith of being a part of one. And she did not help herself in this matter, as she was often outspoken against the occupying force.

Eventually she was given away by a collaborator by the name of Gaston Quien. Edith was arrested on the 3rd August 1915 and held at Saint-Gilles prison for ten weeks. The day before her trial she made a statement admitting to helping 60 British soldiers, 15 French troops and over 100 French and Belgian civilians escape to Holland.

A court martial found her guilty and sentenced her to death. News of this reached the Allies and strong diplomatic pleas were made for mercy and to have the sentence commuted. This was instigated by the USA who had not at this time entered the war. The British government knew that if they did likewise, the German High Council would not view it well and possibly make Edith's position even more precarious.

Unfortunately all attempts failed and at 7am on the 12th October 1915, Edith was executed by firing squad. Her death caused an outrage in the British and foreign press. Germany was condemned for barbarism. Edith was buried locally but after the war her body was brought back to England and buried in Norwich Cathedral. This was not normally allowed but special permission was given by the King himself.

Over the past decades there has been much discussion as to Edith's true activities. The Germans did not execute her for espionage but for treason. So it raises the question – was

Edith working for the Secret Intelligence Service or SIS as well as her other activities? Some believe that she might have started out as a spy for Britain but changed the focus of her work when she began helping the Allied soldiers to escape. She may possibly have decided that this was a more fitting way to satisfy her sense of what was right.

In 2015, the ex-head of the Security Service or MI5 – Stella Rimington – stated that she had seen a Belgium document from that time that hinted that Edith did carry out intelligence work for the Allies. This may be true but it is also important to point out that to date, there has been no conclusive evidence as to which argument is correct. But there is one thing I think that can be agreed upon – she lived and died a heroine.

Statue to the memory of Edith Cavell

Alexander Fleming

Address: 20A Danvers Street, London SW3

Station: Sloane Square Tube

It is true to say that Alexander Fleming's work has probably saved thousands if not millions of lives over the decades. Why? Because his work as a biologist, pharmacologist and botanist resulted in the discovery in 1928 of Penicillin – the first of the anti-biotic drugs used to combat bacterial infections.

Fleming discovered Penicillin

Fleming was born on the 6th August 1881 in Ayrshire in Scotland. His father was a farmer who died when Fleming was only seven years old. His early education took place in local schools until he won a scholarship to Kilmarnock Academy. He then moved to London where he enrolled at the Royal Polytechnic Institution.

He left the institution at the age of sixteen and got a job working in a shipping office. He stayed there for a few years until he came into some money left to him by an uncle. He elder brother Tom suggested he should invest the money in more training and become a doctor like him. So Fleming entered St Mary's Hospital Medical School in Paddington, west London. In 1906 he graduated with distinction.

He first became a bacteriologist working in immunology and researching vaccines. Two years later he gained a degree in bacteriology and became a lecturer at St Mary's. During the First World War he served with distinction in the Army Medical Core with the rank of Captain. Often located in Field Hospitals close to the front line, it was a place you learned to practice surgery as well as other life-saving procedures very quickly.

Fleming returned to St Mary's after the cessation of hostilities in 1918 and continued his research into anti-bacterial agents. During this period he noted that mucus from a patient with a heavy cold had some effect on slowing down bacterial growth. Unfortunately the active agent within the mucus would prove to have no therapeutic value to patients but he was on the right track.

Ten years after returning to St Mary's he made his breakthrough discovery – pretty much by accident. Although acknowledged as a brilliant researcher, Fleming was not as fastidious when it came to keeping his laboratory clean and organised. In 1928 he went away on holiday with his family for the whole of the month of August. When he returned he noticed that a stack of culture dishes containing the bacteria staphylococci which he had left unwashed had grown a fungus. On closer inspection Fleming noticed that one of the dishes containing the fungus seemed to have had an effect on the bacteria – it had died off.

He is then said to have made a remark which turned out to be quite a big understatement. "That's funny," he said. But it was to be more than funny. Investigations showed the fungus to be a form of Penicillin. Further research then uncovered its ability to kill off bacteria associated with a number of deadly conditions such as pneumonia, scarlet fever, diphtheria and meningitis.

However the discovery was not an overnight success – in fact Fleming worked on refining it for the next ten years. He found that it was very difficult to mass produce and in 1940 he concluded his work into it. What he said was needed was a talented chemist who could take the project forward. Two researchers in Oxford took up the challenge and with funding from both the British and American governments, were able to find a way to mass produce the first anti-biotic medication.

Today there are many types of antibiotics and they have saved millions of lives. However there are signs that some bacteria are becoming immune to the drugs and further research is now underway to find new variations. Although Fleming did not find a way to make his discovery available to patients he is credited with its discovery. And for that he earned the 1945 Nobel Prize for Medicine which was presented to him in Sweden by King Gustaf V.

Fleming lived and died here

Ten years after receiving this honour Fleming died of a heart attack. He was at his London home at the time in Chelsea. The date was the 11th March 1955. He left a wife,

Sarah and a son Robert. Unfortunately at the time the picture was taken, the house was undergoing renovation.

Sigmund Freud

Address: 20 Maresfield Gardens, London NW3

Station: Hampstead Tube

Sigmund Freud is probably one of the best-known names in psychology and neurology. Perhaps his main claim to fame was that he founded the subject of psychoanalysis. Although there were and still are a lot of detractors, students of psychology still study the subject and some use aspects of it in their therapy work.

Freud was born in the town of Freiberg in Moravia which is now part of the Czech Republic on the 6th May 1856. His father was a merchant and came from Jewish descent. After moving to Leipzig, the family eventually settled in Vienna where Freud enrolled at the university to study medicine.

After he graduated he worked at the Vienna General Hospital where he began to use the therapeutic procedure of clinical hypnosis in order to treat patients presenting with symptoms of hysteria. He would put them into a trance state and then ask them to recall any painful or traumatic incidents from their past which might have a bearing on their current condition. This is one of the techniques still used by professional hypnotherapists today.

In order to pursue his interests in this area of work, Freud moved to Paris for a year to study under the famous neurologist Jean Charcot. Upon his return, he set up his own private practice in Vienna primarily to treat nervous and hysteric disorders.

Over the following years Freud began to explore the human personality in more detail and sought to form his own theory. He came to believe that within each of us there is an unconscious mind. This is a perfectly rational model understood by therapists today.

However, he went further and postulated that within the unconscious mind there were sexual and aggressive impulses continually at odds with each other.

He then reasoned that the desires and conflicts within the mind could be accessed by interpreting the dreams of his patients. In 1900 he published his research into this area in the book "The Interpretation of Dreams." There were many in the medical world who disagreed with his findings but it didn't seem to affect his standing as two years after publication of this book, Freud was made Professor of Neuropathology at the University of Vienna.

Final home of Sigmund Freud

But not everyone found fault with his theories – there were a number of professionals who came together to form the International Psychoanalytic Association. Its first president was another famous name from psychology – Carl Jung. Eventually Jung would resign the presidency and move away in order to work on his own theories of the human psyche.

Freud continued in his attempts to model the mind and in 1923 he produced a new version. In this one he divided the mind up into three distinct areas – the Id, the Ego and the Superego. He published this new material in a book entitled "The Ego and the Id."

Another group of people who were not impressed with Freud's work were the Nazi Party and in 1933, a number of his books – along with many other titles – were publicly burned. The darkening clouds of World War II were approaching and being of Jewish decent, Freud and his family moved from Vienna and set up home in London.

Freud's house is now a museum

Freud had married Martha Bernays in 1886 and the union produced six children. But Freud's time was beginning to run out – 1923 he had been diagnosed with cancer of the jaw. This had resulted in him undergoing over thirty operations to try to cure the condition – they didn't. Freud died in London on the 23rd September 1939.

Florence Nightingale

Address: 10 South Street, London W1

Station: Green Park Tube

Florence Nightingale is possibly the most famous nurse of all time. She made her name in the Crimean War and was dubbed "the Lady of the Lamp" by the media of the time. But there was much more to her than this. She was also a social reformer and is acknowledged as the founder of modern nursing.

She was born on the 12th May 1820 in Florence, Italy to a rich and well-connected British family. She was named after the place of her birth. A year after she was born the family moved back to England and Florence was brought up in homes in Hampshire and Derbyshire. Her education came mainly from her father and at eighteen he took the whole family on a grand tour of Europe.

As might be imagined, the role expected of Florence was to be married to someone from a good family and to devote her life to being a wife and mother. Unfortunately for her family Florence had other ideas. She was fairly religious and had long held a belief that she was being called to help others. Nursing became the focus of this interest and when she was twenty four made her intentions known to her family – it did not go down well with her mother and sister.

But Florence would not be pushed off track and she began teaching herself as much as she could about the art and science of nursing. However it did not stop her family from trying to get her married off. Florence had one suitor – the poet and politician Richard Milnes - who spent nine years trying to win her hand but eventually she rejected him in favour of her vocation. She travelled across Europe making acquaintances with people who would later help her in her work. These places included Greece and Egypt. But it was in Germany where she spent four months training in nursing practice that gave her life direction. It prompted her to write her first article anonymously on the work she witnessed being carried out there.

Building she lived in is undergoing major maintenance

When she returned to England she took up the post of superintendent at the Institute for the Care of Sick Gentlewomen. It was located in central London at Upper Harley Street. Her father must have supported her career choices for he gave her a private income of £500 per year which allowed her to live comfortably and concentrate on her work. In October 1853 the Crimean War broke out and soon reports began to emerge of the terrible conditions the wounded soldiers had to endure. When Florence heard this she was moved to do something about it. She gathered together thirty eight volunteer nurses and on the 21st October 1854, they were sent by the government to the war zone.

They arrived at Selimiye Barracks in the November and found conditions to be every bit as dire as they had heard. There was very little sanitation which had the result of causing many infections. These would often be the cause of death rather than the original wound. There was very little in the way of medicines available and what was worse, the authorities in charge didn't seem to care what happened to the wounded.

Florence immediately decided something had to be done. And she knew how to put pressure on the government by using the media. She wrote to The Times pleading for the government to help improve the situation of the troops. It worked and none other than Isambard Kingdom Brunel, the famous engineer was brought in to help. He came up with the design of a prefabricated hospital which was then transported out to the Crimea.

It was called the Renkioi Hospital and was run by Dr Alexander Parkes. Within a short time deaths in hospital had been cut by a staggering 90%. Florence introduced such basic hygiene procedures as frequent washing of hands. Figures showed that her changes reduced the death rate from 42% to just 2%.

During the war she became known as The Lady of the Lamp. This was due to an article published in The Times newspaper. It read, "She is a "ministering angel" without any exaggeration in these hospitals, and as her slender form glides quietly along each corridor, every poor fellow's face softens with gratitude at the sight of her. When all the medical officers have retired for the night and silence and darkness have settled down upon those miles of prostrate sick, she may be observed alone, with a little lamp in her hand, making her solitary rounds."

On the 29th November 1855 the Nightingale Fund was set up with the aim of training nurses. Soon the fund had over £45,000 at its disposal and the first training school was opened at St Thomas's Hospital in London on the 9th July 1860. It is now known as The Florence Nightingale School of Nursing and Midwifery and is based within King's College in London.

Florence never married and it has been discussed whether she had any serious relationships in her life. Some believe that her religious drive to do good for others kept her chaste. She had a long life and when she eventually died at the age of 90, it was quietly whilst asleep in her home at 10 South Street, London. The date was the 13th

August 1910. A grateful nation wanted to bury her in Westminster Abbey but her relatives insisted that it should be closer to the family home of Embley Park in Hampshire.

Plaque to Florence Nightingale

Henry Wellcome

Address: 6 Gloucester Gate, London NW1

Station: Camden Town Tube

Henry Wellcome was a pharmaceutical entrepreneur who left a legacy to mankind in the form of one of the largest charitable trusts in the world. He was also an avid collector of all things medical and some of his collection can still be viewed at The Wellcome Collection in London. It is well worth the effort.

Henry was an American and was born on the 21st August 1853 in a log cabin in Wisconsin, USA. His father was a missionary who travelled around the country in a covered wagon. As such Henry was brought up to respect his religious roots. But he was also an entrepreneur at heart and even at the age of sixteen he was selling his own brand of invisible ink. In actual fact this was nothing more than lemon juice but it worked. His other interest was medicine and by combining the two, he was able to form a large pharmaceutical company in later life.

This began in 1880 when, with his business partner – Silas Burroughs – they formed a pharmaceutical company called Burroughs, Wellcome & Company. They brought some new innovations to the industry including medicines in tablet form. Up until that time most medications were dispensed in the form of powders or liquids. In addition they began to market their products directly to doctors and in a stroke of good advertising, sent free samples for them to try out. It worked and the company flourished.

The partnership was not to last too long as Burroughs died at the early age of forty eight. Wellcome took over full control and the business continued to grow. He diversified their drug selling business by setting up research laboratories to investigate new medicines. In 1924 all these business concerns were brought together under one holding – The Wellcome Foundation Ltd.

Magnificent home of Sir Henry Wellcome

He married once – Gwendoline Barnardo of the Barnardo Homes fame - and had one child – Henry - but the union was not a success. Their child was often unwell and since they travelled a great deal, they had him sent to foster parents at the age of three. I must admit this does sound unkind for someone producing products to reduce suffering.

They separated in 1909 and Gwendoline – known by one of her other names, Syrie – had a couple of high profile affairs. One was allegedly with Harry Selfridge – the store magnate – and the other with the author Somerset Maugham with whom she had a daughter. Henry obtained a divorce. He did not like the publicity associated with the case but he did win custody of their son.

Over the years Henry had much of his work centred in Britain and in 1910 he became a British citizen and in 1932 was made a Knight of the Realm. He was also made an honorary member of the Royal College of Surgeons based in Lincoln's Inn Fields. In 1936 he went into hospital for an operation. Whilst there he developed pneumonia from which he died on the 25th July. He was eighty two years old.

He foundered the Wellcome Trust & Foundation

But his work was to be carried on and the Wellcome Trust was established. His company had now been taken in by Glaxo Smith Kline or GSK. Money from this sale went towards the trust. Today it is worldwide and helping to fund research in many areas of medical science. The Wellcome Collection houses some of his collection of artefacts known as the "Medicine Man" collection. At one time it was estimated to contain over 125,000 objects. His legacy has done much good and continues to do so.

Part Five
Soldiers & Sailors

Robert Baden-Powell

Address: 9 Hyde Park Gate, London SW7

Station: Gloucester Road Tube

Robert Baden-Powell had a distinguished military career but he will be best remembered for instigating the Scout Movement which still flourishes today. But for all his success, as a youngster, he was not judged to be academic. BP as Baden-Powell was known for most of his life was born in Paddington, west London on the 22nd February 1857. He was educated at the famous public school Charterhouse in Surrey and then applied to the Army. He passed the selection process – coming in second amongst hundreds of other applicants.

Statue of Baden-Powell

As a young army officer BP was posted to India in 1876 serving with the 13th Hussars. It was here that he specialised in map-making, reconnaissance and as a sign to the future – scouting techniques. He was so successful that he began to instruct other soldiers in the same procedures. This was a new concept for the army and involved working in small units under one leader. Another innovation that BP introduced was the awarding of his own person badges to the soldiers who had done well. The badge awarded incorporated a northerly pointing compass point which would resemble the universal scouting badge of today.

Later his army career would take him to Malta, the Balkans and South Africa. And it would be in various tours of the latter that would earn BP national recognition. He saw action during the Zulu Wars of the late 1870s in the Natal region of the country. But it would be at the end of the nineteenth century during the Boer War that BP would come to prominence.

He found himself as commander of the garrison stationed in the town of Mafeking. Their job was to guard the large quantity of stores in the town. The Boers surrounded them and laid siege. It is said that BP could have destroyed the stores and made an escape through the Boer lines – but he chose to stay and defend the town. The siege lasted for 217 days and by the time they were relieved, they had almost reached the point of having to eat their own horses.

Many stories of Mafeking have been told over the years – many good, some not so. But it does appear that BP used many of his "scouting" techniques to confuse and attack the enemy which at one time was estimated to have numbered over 8,000. BP himself would conduct many of the reconnaissance patrols near the enemy positions and on one occasion he discovered that the railway line was still intact. Upon returning to the town he loaded up an armoured locomotive with soldiers and sent it into the Boer camp. The enemy were caught off-guard and BP scored another success.

When the relief column arrived on the 16th May 1900, BP returned to Britain and found himself hailed as a hero. It also brought him a promotion to Major-General. His next job was to organise the South African Constabulary. But in between these events King Edward VII made him a knight. In 1903 he was made Inspector-General of Cavalry. Once again he was able to employ his scouting procedures into the training of the soldiers. He had also in the past written a book – "Aids to Scouting" – which had been taken up by civilian teachers to instruct their charges in observation and woodwork.

Home of Baden-Powell is just off Hyde Park

BP resigned his commission in 1910 in order to spend his time building the Scouting Movement. When the First World War broke out in 1914, BP offered his services to Lord Kitchener who replied he was more valuable leading the scouts. However, there are reports that BP was actively used during WWI as a spy but we cannot be sure of this.

The Scout Movement could be said to have started with the first camping expedition which was held on Brownsea Island off Poole in Dorset in 1907. It consisted of twenty two boys from various backgrounds who worked together under the leadership of BP. A year later BP's second book "Scouting for Boys" was published. It was a huge success. The Scouting Movement was now a force in itself.

Scouting – the legacy of Baden-Powell

Regarding BP's personal life, he married Olave Soames on the 30th October 1912 in a private service. At the time he was 55 and she was 23 years of age. But the marriage was on the outside a success and they had three children. It is said that each scout donated one penny in order to buy the couple a wedding present. It was also from this time onwards that BP began to suffer from headaches which were considered to be psychosomatic in nature.

In 1939 they moved from their Hampshire home to Kenya where they became part of the Happy Valley sect. But it was not to last for long. BP died there on the 8th January 1941 – he was aged 83. He is buried at St Peter's Cemetery in Nyeri. When Olive passed away in Britain her ashes were brought back to Kenya and interred next to her husband. The tomb is now classed as a national monument by the Kenyan government.

The Scouting Movement is now a world-wide organisation and although BP earned many awards and honours during his lifetime and after his death, it is perhaps the best example of what he was really passionate about. And he is still held in high regard by many people, for in 2002 he came 13th in the BBC list of 100 Greatest Britons and this was the vote of a nationwide public.

William Bligh

Address: 100 Lambeth Road, London SE1

Station: Lambeth North Tube

Captain William Bligh was an officer in the Royal Navy. In addition he was also an explorer and a very talented navigator. However he has gone down in history as the Master of HMS Bounty when her crew mutinied in the South Pacific.

Captain William Bligh RN – Commander HMS Bounty

He was born we believe in Plymouth on the 9th September 1754. His father was associated with seafaring in so much as he was a customs officer. Bligh entered service in the Royal Navy at sixteen with the training rank of midshipman. After six years he was promoted to sailing master and joined the crew of the ship Resolution under the command of one of Britain's best known commanders – Captain James Cook.

It was Cook's third and what would turn out to be his last voyage to the South Pacific. They set sail in 1776 and returned to England three years later without Cook. He had been killed in an altercation with natives in the South Seas. Bligh had learned much during the voyage but he decided his future lay in merchant shipping. He resigned his commission with the Royal Navy and set his sights on sailing in the West Indies.

This was also the period he met and later married Elizabeth Bentham. Although his job meant that he would be away for many years, they set up home in Lambeth, south London at 100 Lambeth Road. The house is still there and it can be easily found as it is opposite the Imperial War Museum. The union produced four daughters – they also had twin sons but they died in infancy.

The Bligh's family home in Southwark

Around 1787 there was a request from some of the plantation owners in the Caribbean for a new staple and cheap foodstuff which they could feed to the slaves working on their plantations. The botanist – Sir Joseph Banks – who incidentally had sailed with Cook on one of his earlier voyages, suggested the answer might be found in breadfruit which was available on the South Pacific island of Tahiti.

It is reported the Admiralty was not very enthusiastic about the project but they made available a ship of 215 tons which was renamed the Bounty for the trip. William Bligh was offered the position of Captain which he accepted. So he was recommissioned back into the Navy.

The Bounty left port on her mission in December 1787. It wasn't long before there was friction between Bligh, his officers and the deckhands. Bligh viewed his officers as lazy and incompetent. This included his first mate and second-in-command – Fletcher Christian. They in turn thought his manner to be distant and aloof. It was also said that Bligh could be verbally abusive to both his officers and men.

However, it is important to point out that reports that he was violent and used corporal punishment regularly are pretty much untrue. In hindsight it has been shown he used physical punishment less than most of his fellow captains of the time.

HMS Bounty made her way to Tahiti via the Cape of Good Hope – the bad weather and violent seas of Cape Horn proved too much for that route to be sailed. They reached their destination and dropped anchor in October 1788. To complete their mission, it would not be a case of jumping ashore, collecting breadfruit, loading it up and then heading back to England. They first had to make sure the plants would survive the voyage. This required them to spend five months on Tahiti readying their cargo for transportation.

One of Bligh's reports states that he believed it was the hedonistic and loose morals of the local inhabitants that had a detrimental effect on his crew and this might have sown the seeds of mutiny. This is still a cause for debate. But by the time they came to leave Tahiti the mood between Bligh and the crew had worsened. The ship set sail for home on the 4th April 1789.

However, it wasn't long before matters came to a head. Fletcher Christian who had been a long-term friend of Bligh's had had enough of what he believed to be the unnecessary torment levelled at him by his captain. He set upon a plan to desert the ship and escape aboard a raft. News of his plan reached the ears of some of his crewmates and they cautioned him against it. Unfortunately, they had him sign up to a new plan – to mutiny and take control of the ship.

Mutiny was a crime punishable by death. However, on the 28th April 1789, they took action along with the Bounty. Bligh and eighteen of his crew who remained loyal to him were put aboard the ship's launch which measured approximately six metres in length. It wasn't much more than a rowing boat which was open to the weather. They were given five days' supply of food and a few basic navigational instruments and then cast away from the ship.

Bligh guided them to the volcanic island of Tofua but when they encountered a local tribe of native islanders, there was a fight which left one of the crew dead. This made up Bligh's mind – he would take the launch and his men to the island of Timor. This was a staggering 3,600 miles away. And the even more amazing thing was – they made it alive, making land on the 14th June 1789. It is still regarded in many circles to have been one of the greatest feats of navigation in maritime history. From here they made their way to Java and to what is now the capitol of Indonesia – Jakarta. Here they were able to find passage back to England.

As for the Bounty, it first made its way back to Tahiti where three of the mutineers elected to stay. The rest of the crew under the command of Fletcher Christian sailed to the island of Pitcairn which they made their home - for they knew they could never return to England.

When Bligh reached the Admiralty – arriving in March 1790 – he was absolved of all blame and a ship named the Pandora was dispatched to track down the mutineers. Three of them were captured on Tahiti and returned to England. In the meantime, Bligh was given another ship to command. But whilst he was away, rumours and accusations arose concerning his part in the mutiny. These defamations were to follow and hound him and his reputation for the rest of his life.

Nevertheless, he still had a full career in the Navy commanding a number of ships. He even served as Governor of New South Wales from 1805 to 1810. Admiral Lord Nelson commended him for the part he played in the Battle of Camperdown in 1797. He also returned to the South Pacific on a number of occasions and is credited with discovering thirteen new islands.

William Bligh died on the 7th December 1817. He is buried in a church which is now the Museum of Gardening. It is next door to Lambeth Palace, the London home of the Archbishop of Canterbury. His tomb is quite impressive and is located in the centre of the churchyard.

Hugh Dowding

Address: 3 St Mary's Road, London SW19

Station: Wimbledon Tube

Many people are aware of "The Few" as Prime Minister Winston Churchill called the Spitfire and Hurricane pilots of the Battle of Britain which took place during the summer and autumn of 1940. But less know that one of the main architects behind their victory was Hugh Dowding.

He was born on the 24th April 1882 in the southern Scotland town of Moffat. His father was a teacher and had taught at the famous school of Fettes College in Edinburgh. Dowding was first educated locally at St Ninian's School in Moffat and then at Winchester College. He joined the Army at eighteen and did his initial training at the Royal Military Academy at Woolwich, south east London.

He served in many parts of the world including Hong Kong, Ceylon (now Sri Lanka), Gibraltar and India. Dowding was promoted to the rank of captain on the 18th August 1913 and was posted to the Isle of Wight. He was about to reach a turning point that would help to mark out his future career. Dowding had developed an interest in aviation and on the 19th December 1913 he obtained his Aviator's Certificate – numbered 711 – on a Vickers School of Flying biplane stationed at Brooklands Aerodrome.

From here he went to the Central Flying School where he was awarded his coveted "wings". He then returned to his Army duties but the lure of a flying career was too strong and so in August 1914, he joined the Royal Flying Core as a pilot with No. 7 Squadron. He saw action in France serving with No. 6 Squadron before becoming the commanding officer with No. 16 Squadron in July 1915. By August 1917 he had been promoted to commander of the Southern Training Brigade. With the conclusion of the First World

War, the hectic life of Dowding normalised and he was granted a permanent commission in the newly formed Royal Air Force on the 1st August 1919. He now had the rank of Group Captain.

On the 16th February 1918 he married Clarice Vancourt. They had one son whom they named Derek. Following the death of Clarice, Dowding married again – this time to Muriel Whiting. The marriage took place on the 25th September 1951. They had no children.

During the 1920s he served in Iraq, Jorden and Palestine. By 1930, he was back in Britain as Air Member for Supply & Research. It was during this tour that he granted an airworthiness certificate to the R101 airship. It crashed on its maiden voyage to India. Dowding regretted his decision to sign off the aircraft and wished instead that he had insisted on more testing beforehand.

Dowding led Fighter Command during the Battle of Britain

In 1936 his career began to take the form that would eventually make him one of the main focuses during the Battle of Britain for he was put in charge of Fighter Command.

114

The reason that the Battle of Britain took place was for control of the airspace above southern Britain. The German Army were massed on the French side of the Channel ready to invade. But first, they had to destroy the RAF. In the words of Churchill, "Never was so much owed by so many to so few." The pilots who defended the skies are justly honoured.

But there was another crucial factor in the battle and that was termed the "Dowding system". It was founded on creating an integrated defence system which had a number of distinct parts to it. The first was to fully utilise the capabilities of a new invention – radar. And because it was so new, it still needed some refinements – for instance the equipment was not very accurate at gauging altitudes. So the second segment of the system was to incorporate the human element in the form of the Royal Observer Core whose members informed command of any enemy aircraft approaching the shores.

The third part was termed raid plotting which meant producing a board on which enemy groups could be placed in relation to their strength, position, direction and altitude. This meant that squadrons could then be tasked to intercept them before they reached their targets. Finally, aircraft pilots needed to be able to talk to each other and communicate with the ground controllers. So aircraft radio production was given a high priority.

All of these factors were controlled from RAF Bentley Priory. There was also one other important element to the system and that was of course the aircraft and pilots. Dowding oversaw that the production of Spitfires and Hurricanes was as good as could be. He was also instrumental in insisting that the cockpit canopies were constructed to be bullet resistant – something every pilot was grateful for.

During the battle itself, Dowding allowed his commanders to run the battle in detail but in the background he was working hard to obtain a victory. He reasoned that to get that victory he had to ensure that there were enough pilots and aircraft available to cover losses due to enemy action. He also ensured that he kept back sufficient reserves of aircraft and pilots until circumstances would force them to be used. By the end of autumn 1940 the battle was won and the threat of invasion retreated. Dowding was credited for getting the victory.

However the episode was not all plain sailing. All along, Dowding faced opposition from a number of his senior officers who believed his Fabian System was not the best way to fight the Luftwaffe. They preferred the idea of large set-piece air battles called the Big Wing. Although Dowding won out, he came under a lot of flak soon after the battle. It resulted in his retirement which he felt was forced upon him. He stepped down on the 24th November 1940. It was to leave him feeling bitter for the rest of his life.

Dowding's original house is no longer there

Between 1941 and 1951 he lived in Wimbledon. The original house is no longer there but a plaque still commemorates him. Hugh Dowding died on the 15th February 1970 at his home in Royal Tunbridge Wells in Kent. His ashes were laid below the Battle of Britain memorial window in Westminster Abbey.

T.E. Lawrence

Address: 14 Barton Street, London SW1

Station: Westminster Tube

The name T.E. Lawrence might not immediately bring to mind who this person was and what effect they had on a certain part of the world. But if we hear the title he was best known as, then most people will know exactly who we are talking about – it is Lawrence of Arabia.

He was Welsh, being born in Tremadog in North Wales on the 16th August 1888. His father came from Ireland and owned an estate in County Westmeath. He was married to Edith and they had four daughters. However, he absconded with the family's governess – Sarah Junner.

Lawrence was the second son born out of wedlock as his father never divorced his wife. This was not viewed well at all at this time and so the family had to keep on the move. The places they spent time in included Scotland, Jersey and France.

In 1896 they arrived in Oxford and Lawrence enrolled in the City of Oxford High School. He was a successful pupil and went on to study history at Jesus College Oxford where he graduated with a first class honours degree.

Lawrence's first foray into the Arab world came in 1909 when he made a 1,000 mile walking tour of Syria in order to study Crusader castles. This led to him being taken on as an archaeologist working in the ancient city of Carchemish. Today it lies close to the border between Turkey and Syria. In addition to this work, he and a fellow archaeologist – Leonard Woolley – made a survey of the Sinai Desert. Their work was published as "The Wilderness of Zin."

Lawrence's excavations were cut short by the outbreak of the First World War. He was commissioned as a second lieutenant. Because of his knowledge and experience in the Middle East, he was stationed in Cairo, Egypt as part of British Military Intelligence. But it would be in October 1916 that he would begin the work that would later come to define him.

Lawrence became the Liaison Officer to Emir Feisal. Feisal and his father had been one of the organising powers behind what became known as the Arab Revolt. This involved the use of Arab irregular troops who conducted guerrilla-style operations against the enemy which in this part of the world was the Ottoman Empire. Lawrence threw himself into the task and soon showed he was a great tactician and understood all the concepts of conducting guerrilla warfare. Turkish supply routes and lines of communications were targeted and destroyed or disrupted. Their first big victory was the seizing of the strategically important town of Aqaba. From here Lawrence and his troops moved north – again finding much success against their foe.

Lawrence's home in London

The result of all this was that the Turks had to redeploy thousands of troops away from the front line in order to try to control a small Arab force. Consequently the allied troops found that their job had become a little easier. But Lawrence was driven by more than military victories. He was looking into the future when the war would be over. He envisaged a land where the Arabs once again would be in charge and govern their own lands.

With the fall of Damascus, Lawrence set off for Paris to attend the Peace Conference being held there. He intended to push for Arab independence but when he arrived he found that the British and French governments had already settled on who was to rule and it wasn't going to be the Arabs.

Lawrence wasn't beaten and he used his own fame and celebrity status he had achieved in war to carry on his mission. This was also the time that he began to record his adventures in a book which would eventually become a classic of its type – the "Seven Pillars of Wisdom."

In 1921 Winston Churchill appointed him to the position of Advisor on Arab Affairs at the Colonial Office. A new peace conference was arranged. It was to be held in Cairo and resulted in a new map of the Middle Easy being drawn up which remains pretty much the same to this day.

But for Lawrence the high-profile celebrity status which was accorded to him did not sit comfortably. In order to attempt to escape it he resigned from his government position and enrolled in the Royal Air Force under an assumed name. But his escape from fame did not last long for in 1923 he was discovered, forcing him to leave the RAF. Two months later he enlisted in the Tank Corps as a private soldier. He chose the name of Thomas Shaw in order to keep out of the spotlight.

However, he was unhappy in the Corps and his health began to suffer. In 1925 he re-entered the RAF and was stationed at Cranwell. He was then sent to India and to near the border with Afghanistan. There were some rumours in newspapers that during his time there he had been involved in encouraging insurrection within Afghanistan. But we do not know if this was true.

Upon his return to England he was posted to Plymouth in the south west of the country. He became involved in the preparations to win the Schneider Trophy which was a high-speed seaplane contest. He then began to work on the development of fast rescue boats for the RAF. It was said this came about after he witnessed an RAF flying boat crashing near Plymouth.

Lawrence's life was cut short by a motorbike accident

In early 1935 Lawrence retired from the RAF and settled down at his home in Dorset. But it was not to be a long retirement for in May 1935 he had an accident whilst riding his motorcycle. His machine went out of control when he swerved to avoid two boys riding bicycles. Lawrence died a few days later on the 19th May 1935 – he never regained consciousness. He is buried at Moreton in Dorset.

Louis Mountbatten

Address: 2 Wilton Crescent, London SW1

Station: Hyde Park Corner Tube

Lord Louis Mountbatten had a pretty spectacular military career – he not only witnessed many important events of the twentieth century, he was also instrumental in their instigation. He was also a member of and therefore close to the Royal Family.

Born in Windsor on the 25th June 1900, his full name was Louis Francis Albert Victor Nicholas Battenburg. His father - Prince Louis of Battenburg changed the family's name to Mountbatten in 1917 when he felt that a less German sounding name would be more appropriate.

For much of his young life Mountbatten was educated at home by private tutors. But when he was fourteen he entered the Britannia Royal Naval College at Dartmouth in Devon. This was where Royal Navy officers were and still are given their initial training before entering the service. Mountbatten officially entered the Royal Navy two years later in 1916 and saw action during the last two years of the First World War.

After the war he stayed on in the Navy and in 1934 achieved his first command – HMS Daring, a destroyer. At the outbreak of the Second World War in 1939, Mountbatten was appointed the commander of a fleet of destroyers located in the Mediterranean. However, during an action in 1941, his ship – HMS Kelly – was dive-bombed by enemy aircraft and sunk. Half of his crew were killed in the attack. Incidentally, one of the most famous films of the Second World War – In Which We Serve by Noel Coward – was based on this episode of the war.

In 1942, with D-Day still two years off, Mountbatten was given responsibility for preparing for the invasion. A further promotion followed in 1943 when he was made supreme allied commander of the South East Asia Command. He held this position until after the war and with General Sim, was responsible for halting the Japanese offensive towards India. In September 1945 he received the official surrender of Japanese forces after they had been forced out of Burma.

With the resumption of peace, Mountbatten was appointed viceroy of India with special responsibility for preparing for British withdrawal. He was only partially successful in this endeavour as it led to the partition of India and the creation of the state of Pakistan. Students of history will know that relations between the two countries has been strained ever since.

Belgravia home of the Earl & Countess Mountbatten

This period of government diplomatic service ended in 1953 when he retired from the Royal Navy. He was however given command of the newly created NATO Mediterranean Command. A year later he was appointed as First Sea Lord. There were now only a couple of positions higher than this and in 1959, Mountbatten achieved one of them by becoming Chief of the Defence Staff. In 1965 he retired from service.

For someone who had spent much of his life living in theatres of conflict, it is perhaps not surprising that that he died a violent death. However, it came not from open warfare, but from a hidden bomb prepared by terrorists belonging to the IRA or Irish Republican Army. Mountbatten had a holiday home at Classiebawn Castle in the Republic of Ireland. On the 27th August 1979 he was aboard his boat off the coast of County Sligo. With him were two relatives and a local lad who was just fifteen years old. The bomb went off and all of them were killed.

Mountbatten had a distinguished career

Mountbatten's funeral service was held at Westminster Cathedral and was followed by a burial at Romsey Abbey on the south coast of England.

Part Six
Novelists

Jane Austen

Address: 10 Henrietta Street, London WC2

Station: Covent Garden Tube

Jane Austen is one of the best-known English female authors of all time. Her six novels have led her to being described as the founder of the modern English novel. It is her depiction of unremarkable and ordinary characters of the middle classes and country society in their day to day life that made her work so unique for its time. But it would not be until her death that she would become acknowledged - for most of her work was published anonymously.

She was born on the 16th December 1775 in the village of Steventon in the county of Hampshire. Her father was the Reverend George Austen and she was one of two daughters and six brothers. Although she wrote of love and relationships, she and her sister Cassandra did not marry. But her early family life was a happy one, with her mother writing verses and always encouraging the family to play act. It was an environment that led her to begin to observe and write about the local characters that she knew on the estate and from the villages around.

Her first forays into writing are contained within three collections of short stories, prose and plays entitled Volume the First, Second and Third. It was in 1795 that Jane began her first novel – Sense and Sensibility. Her father put it forward for publication but it was declined. Up to this point Jane felt that the stability she had in life helped her in her writing but this was to change when in 1801, her father decided to move and retire to Bath. This had the consequence that Jane ended up living in a number of places – all of them temporary homes. Their locations included London, Clifton, Bath, Warwickshire and Southampton.

One of her many homes was in London

This disruption in her life ended in 1809 when her brother – Edward – was able to provide accommodation for both sisters and their mother. It was in a cottage on an estate in the village of Chawton in Hampshire. Her father was not able to join them as he had died four years earlier.

10 Henrietta Street today

Feeling more settled Jane set about reviving and revising her writing. Both Sense and Sensibility and Pride and Prejudice were completed and made ready for publication. Another brother – Henry – acted as an agent for her and negotiated with various publishers. In 1811 the publisher Thomas Egerton accepted Sense and Sensibility and it was published anonymously. It received positive critical reviews. Pride and Prejudice followed in 1813 – again through Thomas Egerton. Mansfield Park was published a year later. Although all these books did well, no one knew the identity of the author. From 1813 to 1814 she lived at 10 Henrietta Street in Covent Garden.

In December 1815, Emma was published by the famous London-based publisher John Murray who also published the works of Lord Byron. He also published two of Jane's books posthumously – Persuasion and Northanger Abbey. As an aside, Murray was responsible for the burning of Byron's diaries after the poet's death. He believed that their frank content was too racy for the general readership to endure. So they were burned in his upstairs office. Incidentally, although John Murray has been taken over by another publisher, the office building in Mayfair is still there.

Original Office of John Murray

It was in January 1816 that the first symptoms of the illness which would eventually kill Jane were noticed. She believed that she was suffering from "bile" but some modern clinicians think that she had contracted Addison's disease. Gradually over 1816 and into the following year, her health declined. In the April of 1817 Jane made out her Last Will and Testament.

On the 18th July 1817, Jane passed away and was buried at Winchester Cathedral. It was perhaps left to the likes of Sir Walter Scott and the theologian Richard Whately to bring the name of Jane Austen into public awareness. Scott reviewed Emma and said that this nameless author was a master exponent of the modern novel. Whately reviewed Persuasion and Northanger Abbey in 1821. These favourable reviews led to Jane becoming known as the author of these works and then to be considered as a serious author of great standing, which is how we look on her today.

Arthur Conan-Doyle

Address: 2 Upper Wimpole Street, London W1

Station: Regent's Park Tube

Sir Arthur Conan-Doyle was a writer originating from Scotland who above all other things will be remembered for the creation of one particular fictional character – perhaps the most famous detective of all time. He is of course Sherlock Holmes and he has featured in many books, films and TV series over the years. And it is true to say that he is today, more popular than ever.

Residence of Sir Arthur Conan-Doyle

But turning back to his creator, Conan-Doyle was born in Edinburgh on the 22nd May 1859. He was the second of ten children and he spent his early education in Lancashire before spending a year in Austria. When he returned to Edinburgh he enrolled in the University of Edinburgh Medical School where some years later he graduated as a doctor. It was while he was studying there that he noticed the perfection and attention to detail his tutor – Dr Joseph Bell – paid to his patients when assessing their condition. This exacting observation sparked in him the idea of a detective being able to deduce answers from available evidence.

Sherlock Holmes made his first appearance in Beeton's 1887 Christmas Annual in the story entitled "A Study in Scarlet." Because of the books' success with the public he continued to write about Holmes until 1926. But the fame derived from the books was a two edged sword for Conan-Doyle. He expressed a view that they overshadowed his other work to the extent that they did not get a fair hearing. I personally think this is true as some of his other works are notable. These include "The Lost World" where Professor Challenger and his team go in search of a land still inhabited by dinosaurs. Once again this idea has been copied many times by other authors and film-makers.

Conan-Doyle worked from his home in London

The characters of Holmes and Challenger rely on scientific evidence in their work. We find Challenger sceptical of living dinosaurs until he actually sees one. And Holmes would often spot the truth when it was hidden from plain view by examining the evidence presented. This is interesting for if we examine the life of Conan-Doyle we find that he shared a view that relied on belief rather than the scientific method. This came about through his interest in spiritualism. He strongly believed that departed spirits could return and communicate with the living.

To this end he wrote a number of books in an attempt to rationalise the subject to the general public. Through these works he was eventually to become one of the leading authorities on the subject. However he lost a lot of his believers when he wrote two books which held that fairies really existed. In a famous event which later turned out to be faked, two young girls were photographed with fairies at the bottom of their garden. It appears that Conan-Doyle was duped by the pictures and lost a lot of credibility with his supporters.

In addition to these books and his other works of fiction, he also produced a number of non-fiction titles on subjects such as military campaigns and true crime. On the personal side of his life Conan-Doyle married twice. The first was in 1885 to Louisa Hawkins – they had two children. Louisa died in 1906 and a year later he married Jean Leckie – she bore him another three children. Sir Arthur Conan-Doyle died at his home in Crowborough on the 7th July 1930 but his characters will continue to live on.

Charles Dickens

Address: 48 Doughty Street, London WC1

Station: Chancery Lane Tube

Charles Dickens is acknowledged by most to be one of the greatest English writers that has lived. Not only did he create characters and stories which held the public imagination, he also described London in so much detail that it could be said that his books are a social history of Victorian London.

One of England's greatest novelists

But he was not born in London – in fact he was born in Portsmouth in Hampshire on the 7th February 1812. Portsmouth has always been famous for its dockyards and his father was employed there as a pay clerk. In 1815 his job was transferred to London and so the family including three year old Charles moved to the capitol. Two years later they moved again – this time to Chatham, another naval dockyard, where Charles began his education. It was interrupted in 1822 when once again, they moved back to London. But his experiences of Chatham and the neighbouring towns of Rochester and Sheerness would aid him in his future writings.

There followed other events which would also colour his work – Dickens began work in 1823 in a blacking factory. At about the same time his father fell into debt and was imprisoned in Marshalsea's debtor's prison. There are still a few remains of the prison which is situated in Southwark and can be viewed today. When his father was released, Dickens was able to finish his basic schooling. He was still only fifteen years of age.

Plaque at the remains of Marshalsea Prison

His next job was working for a firm of solicitors where he impressed and was good at his job. He also became very proficient at writing in shorthand. His writing career proper started in 1829 when he became a journalist and began to write about law cases. Two years later he moved on and became a parliamentary reporter. His first short story was published in 1833. A year later he joined the newspaper The Morning Chronicle.

In 1836 two big events happened in his life – he got married and wrote The Pickwick Papers. This earned him fame and he soon became a household name. But the work was not published as one book. Instead it was published in instalments. Dickens left The Chronicle in 1836 and became editor of Bentley's Miscellany – a magazine. During this period he wrote two of his best-known and loved books – Oliver Twist and Nicholas Nickleby. Another popular novel – The Old Curiosity Shop – followed. There then began a period where his books did not receive the same kind of acceptance that he had enjoyed up to now.

Dickens lived at 48 Doughty Street

In 1842 he visited America and upon returning wrote American Notes for General Circulation – not the snappiest of titles. It did not go down well with readers from both sides of the Atlantic. Barnaby Rudge and Martin Chuzzlewit which were written about the same time were not too popular either. However, this all changed when A Christmas Carol was published in 1843. He was back in demand. From 1846 to 1849 Dickens produced two new novels – Dombey and Son and David Copperfield. His style had changed and these stories were more serious than past ones.

In 1850 he became the joint owner and editor of a weekly magazine called Household Words. He was able to use this journal as a way of bringing three new pieces of work to the public. Each of them is still held in high esteem. They are Bleak House, Hard Times and Little Dorrit. Although his writing career was doing very well the same could not be said of his marriage and in 1858 he and his wife divorced.

A year later he replaced Household Words with a new weekly publication called All The Year Around. Once again he used it to feature his own pieces of new work. They were published in instalments and the first edition began with A Tale of Two Cities. Great Expectations and Our Mutual Friend followed in the same manner.

More and more of his time was now being given over to him making personal reading tours of his books. He travelled to America again to give readings. All of this began to take its toll and his health began to decline. He was writing The Mystery of Edwin Drood when he died on the 9th June 1870. Charles Dickens is buried in Westminster Abbey – a fitting resting place for one of our greatest authors.

Dickens' Museum is next door

If you should visit his house in Doughty Street you will discover that next door – at number 49 - is the Charles Dickens Museum which is open to the public.

Ian Fleming

Address: 22 Ebury Street, London SW1

Station: Victoria Tube

Ian Fleming was a British author who created one of the best-known fictional characters of all time – a spy, licensed to kill, a lover of the high-life, with glamourous women around every corner and a high-tech gadget to get him out of trouble, which was often. From this description it could be none other than "Bond, James Bond."

But it could be argued that his creator led a life which in certain ways outdid Bond. Born on the 28th May 1908 in London, Fleming enjoyed wealth and privilege from a young age. His father was a Conservative Member of Parliament and nothing was spared in giving the young Fleming a good and wide ranging education which encompassed England, Germany and Switzerland.

Many of Bond's villains were based in Russia at the time of the Cold War and it is possible that some of Fleming's background research came from the years – 1929 to 1932 – that he spent in Moscow working as a journalist. This was followed up with terms working as a banker and then as a stockbroker.

When the Second World War broke out in 1939, Fleming was recruited into the military security services – in his case it was Naval Intelligence. He managed to reach a senior position there before the cessation of hostilities.

His next job was as the foreign manager of the London Sunday Times – a position he held until 1949. From this point on Fleming became a full-time author and writer. His first Bond book was published in 1953 and was called Casino Royale. This was followed by a number of well-known 007 titles including From Russia with Love (1957), Dr No (1958), Goldfinger (1959) and Thunderball in 1961.

Fleming's impressive home in London

The Bond novels sold well on both sides of the Atlantic and they received a marketing boost when in 1961 President John F Kennedy included one of them as one of his favoured holiday reads. But it is also true to say that not everyone was a fan. Many literary critics were unimpressed by the writing, the plotlines and the character of Bond himself. Some described him as a sadistic and licensed criminal.

And the funny thing was that Fleming pretty much agreed with their assessment of Bond. He said that he should not be looked upon as a hero but was exactly the sort of person you needed when the going got really tough. Another vocal critic was the Russian government who described the world that Bond inhabited as a place "where laws are written with a pistol barrel."

However, despite these detractors, Fleming went on to write twelve Bond titles. All have been made into films and perhaps one of the greatest accolades to being an actor is to be asked to play the part of 007. In most cases this has led to a career of fame and fortune. These days the movie scripts do not rely on Fleming's original works – and some might say they rarely did – as there are now over twenty Bond films which have grossed over £1 billion.

Fleming may be best known for his Bond novels but he also produced two collections of short stories featuring the spy. However he also wrote a children's book which became a very popular film. It starred a magical flying car and was called "Chitty Chitty Bang Bang." Fleming also wrote in a "supercar" in Goldfinger – the legendary Aston Martin DB5 – I know which one I'd prefer.

Fleming's life mirrored Bond's in some ways

As stated earlier, Fleming's life reflected Bond's in many ways. He mixed with the rich and famous and he also enjoyed danger. Two of his sporting interests were caving and shark hunting. Fleming died on the 12th August 1964 in Canterbury in Kent. Perhaps the best way to sum up his life should be left to the philosophy of one of his characters – Commander Pott – who said of life, "Never say No to adventure. Always say Yes, otherwise you'll lead a very dull life."

Rudyard Kipling

Address: 43 Villiers Street, London WC2

Station: Embankment Tube

Rudyard Kipling was an English novelist, short-story writer and poet who was a man of his time. But perhaps his problem was that he stayed in those times when most other people had begun to move on. He was a person of British Imperialism and it is that which he wrote about and genuinely believed in.

So in a way it is not surprising that he was born in Bombay – now Mumbai – in an India governed by the British on the 30th December 1865. His father was an academic and artist who went on later to become the curator of Lahore Museum – which Kipling called a "wonder house." When he was six years old he was taken back to England. But it was not to live with his parents – instead he was sent to a foster home in Southsea near Portsmouth where he spent five unhappy years. Things did not improve because following this, he was sent to a second-rate public school in Devon. It has been reported that these experiences haunted him for the rest of his life.

At the age of seventeen Kipling returned to India and found work as a journalist. It offered him the opportunity to observe the daily life of India and its people. From these observations he wrote many short pieces and prose. He began to have his work published and collections of prose and short-stories were soon available. Within these books were tales which were to mark him out as a writer including "The Man Who Would Be King" and "Soldiers Three." Kipling's fame began to grow and it wasn't confined to India.

When he returned to England in 1889 he found that he was being acclaimed as one of the foremost prose writers of the period. His new collection of verses were published in 1892 and was called the "Barrack-Room Ballads." They include some titles which are still well-known today such as Gunga Din and Mandalay. It has been said that when Alfred Lord Tennyson died in 1892, many though that Kipling should take his place as the Poet Laureate.

Kipling's London home for two years

That same year Kipling got married to an American Caroline Balestier. They moved to the United States – to Vermont – but they felt they were not welcome and found it hard to settle. This was probably in part due to Kipling's own view of people from other countries. He described Americans as foreigners – no better than the French – and that only "lesser breeds" were born beyond the English Channel. Not the sort of sentiment to endear yourself to your neighbours. And so in 1896 they moved back to England. These years were to see him produce some of his best-known novels. These included Kim, Captains Courageous, the Just So Stories and of course to many people, the most famous of all – The Jungle Book.

It was in 1902 that Kipling moved for the last time – he purchased a house in Burwash in Sussex and he would remain here for the rest of his life. But he was about to earn an award that would forever stand him out as a writer of distinction. In 1907 he was awarded the Nobel Prize for Literature. He would have been even prouder knowing that he was the first Englishman to receive this honour.

As I said at the start of this piece, Kipling was a person who refused to let go of his imperialist views and in fact, in later life they would become even stronger. But by delving deeper into the psyche of the man it is evident that his justification for these views did not lie in racism. He genuinely felt that bringing the culture of England to the masses really helped them. It is an argument which does not stand up to scrutiny especially today, but he was a person who believed he was doing the right thing. He died in London on the 18th January 1936.

Kipling remained a man out of his time

Part Seven

Photographers

Bill Brandt

Address: 4 Airlie Gardens, London W8

Station: Notting Hill Gate Tube

Bill Brandt was born on the 2nd May 1904 in Hamburg, Germany. His father was British and his mother German. He did not have happy memories at school – it was the time of the First World War and his father was interned for six months – and he felt he was being bullied for being half British. He would later put it down to the beginnings of the rise of Nazism within the country. Later he would go much further and renounce his German roots completely and say that he was born in south London.

In the 1920s Brandt was troubled by tuberculosis and received treatment in Switzerland and Vienna. It was whilst he was in Switzerland that he took up photography. He recovered from his affliction and became associated with a Dr Eugenie Schwarzwald. She was a socialite and found him work in a photographic studio. It was whilst working at this studio that Brandt met Eva Boros. They fell in love and were married in Barcelona in 1932.

Schwarzwald also had many social contacts. One of these was the American poet Ezra Pound. Brandt produced a portrait of him and Pound offered him an introduction to the photographic artiste Man Ray who at the time had a studio in Paris. It was 1930 and Brandt worked for him for several months. It was to open his eyes as to the possibilities the medium had to offer.

In 1933 Brandt and Eva moved to London so he could carry on his work as a photographer. They made their home in Belsize Park near Hampstead in north London. Their other address in London was at 4 Airlie Gardens in Notting Hill. He worked for a number of magazines but he also produced a number of photographic books featuring his work. One of these was published in 1936 under the title of "The English at Home." He covered all strata of society and this is illustrated in his first book. The front cover depicts people from the higher levels of society out enjoying themselves whilst the back cover illustrates a poorer family in their modest home.

Brandt's home in Notting Hill

His second book – "A Night in London" – also looked at the differences in the social classes evident at the time. This presented a problem, in as much as he had to take his pictures at night. Film was slow and required artificial lighting to capture images. Brandt used a set of tungsten lamps still called photo-floods to help him in this. Flash systems had been invented but he preferred the steady light of a lamp. Many of the people featured were family or friends of his. So in a way, this was not documentary or pure photojournalism. However, it still made its point.

Within the photographic and film industry there is a term called "day for night" which Brandt would have known. What this means is that either through controlling contrast and exposure when taking the picture or by manipulation of the image later in the darkroom, you can make scenes shot in daytime look as though they were taken at night. It was a very common technique during the early part of the twentieth century and is still used now and again today. At its simplest, you need a bright day with strong shadows and then to underexpose your subject. It is especially effective in black and white photography which Brandt would have been using.

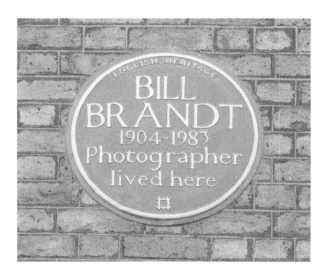

Plaque outside 4 Airlie Gardens

Brandt carried on his interest in recording social issues during the Depression of the 1930s. He chose to travel to the north of Britain where he photographed both the effect it had on industry, the towns and on the people affected by absolute poverty. Brandt described one of his photographs of a man pushing a bicycle with a small bag of coal on it, "He was pushing his bicycle along a footpath through a desolate wasteland between Hebburn and Jarrow. Loaded on the crossbar was a sack of small coal, all that he had found after a day's search on the slag-heaps."

When the Second World War broke out in 1939 Brandt found himself working to record many of the aspects of how the lives of people were affected in London. He covered the ad-hoc bomb shelters that utilised the platforms of the London Underground Stations. People would enter the stations and spend the night there or until the bombing threat had passed. The Ministry of Information commissioned him to cover the London Blitz. To give you an idea of how powerful a photograph can be, some of his pictures of the Blitz were sent to Washington as part of the case for America to enter the war.

After the war Brandt went back to working for a number of magazines. His subjects varied from portraits to landscapes. He would often wait until a scene was right even if it meant waiting months for the correct season and weather conditions. He was to base much of this discipline from Edward Weston – a landscape photographer from California – whom he admired very much. (I have to agree with him as Weston is one of my favourite photographers).

Brandt made various portraits featuring many of the famous people of the time including Dylan Thomas, Francis Bacon, Graham Greene and Robert Graves. He also experimented with the nude form often using a camera equipped with a wide-angle lens for effect.

He continued to work into the latter part of the twentieth century and also lectured at the Royal College of Art. He died on the 20th December 1983 after a short illness.

Terrence Donovan

Address: 30 Bourdon Street, London W1

Station: Bond Street Tube

Terrence Donovan has rightly been named as one of the original celebrity photographers. Together with David Bailey and Brian Duffy they became as big as the rich, famous and glamourous people they portrayed in their pictures. Donovan went on to direct many films – shorts, documentaries, adverts and one movie. But although he was comfortable in the highest of social circles, his early years were anything but glamourous.

He was a real east-end boy being born in Stepney Green on the 14th September 1936. Although at the age of eleven he studied at the London County School of Photoengraving and Lithography, it wasn't until he reached the age of fifteen that he took his first photograph. He left the school and became a photographic assistant in the John French Studio. It was here that he developed his understanding of the medium and within a relatively short time he opened his own studio – he was just twenty two years old.

At the time much of London and certainly most of the east end of London still bore the scars of the Second World War bombings. Half destroyed buildings stood side by side with stark examples of industrial sites. It was the perfect combination for Donovan to use as a backdrop for his subject matter including high fashion. Magazines liked his style and he was soon in great demand.

It was also the time of the "Swinging Sixties" and he found himself at the front line of the fashion and celebrity industries. His clients included Vogue, Harper's Bazaare, Elle and Nova magazines. With Bailey and Duffy they became known as the "Black Trinity" thanks to another photographic great by the name of Norman Parkinson. They moved seamlessly among the top actors, musicians and fashion gurus of the time. Anybody who was anybody wanted to be "shot" by one or all three of them.

In 1978 he moved his studio to a new location – at 30 Bourdon Street in Mayfair. He kept and worked out of it until his death. The same decade also saw Donovan move into film-making. His work began to fall into two distinct areas – he used photography for advertising and fashion projects for the print industry and film for television advertising campaigns. It is estimated that he directed over 3,000 television commercials in his career. He also made a police movie called "Yellow Dog" which did not do terribly well and it is rarely seen today.

Donovan's home and studio in London

There was also a new area of film-making in which Donovan became a pioneer. It is now part and parcel of the pop music industry but when Donovan started, the "pop music video" was a new art-form. Perhaps his best remembered work was for the artiste Robert Palmer for his recording of "Addicted to Love" released in 1986.

His variety of "celebrity" subjects even stretched to the Royal Family and he became a particular favourite of Diana, Princess of Wales. He took her picture on many occasions.

Donovan was a man of many talents – he was a painter and by contrast, a black belt in judo. He married on two occasions – the first was to Janet Cohen but it did not last very long. His second was to Diana Dare and they were still together when he died.

Donovan spent 18 years here

And speaking of his death, it came by his own hand. Despite his fame – or perhaps because of it – he lived with depression for a lot of his life. It eventually got the best of him and he died on the 22nd November 1996 – he was just sixty years old. He left a wife and three children.

Roger Fenton

Address: 2 Albert Terrace, London NW1

Station: Camden Town Tube

Unlike the previous photographer – Terrence Donovan – Roger Fenton was a different kind of picture-taker. For a start he worked in the mid-nineteenth century when photography was still in its infancy. And for Fenton, the main subject of his focus was war photography – in particular the Crimean War.

He was born on the 28th March 1814 in Rochdale, Lancashire. His family was not poor – his father was both a banker and a Member of Parliament. He graduated from Oxford University in 1840 with a degree in English, Maths, Greek and Latin. His intention was to then read law. But he also had a strong interest in painting. This meant that he did not qualify as a solicitor until 1847. During this same period he got married to a lady by the name of Grace Maynard. He also spent much of this time in Paris studying painting under Delaroche amongst others.

But by 1847, Fenton was back in London where he continued his artistic studies under Charles Lucy with whom he would remain friends. He must have had talent as he was soon exhibiting at the Royal Academy. The Great Exhibition of 1851 held in Hyde Park may have been the trigger to his becoming fascinated by the new medium of photography. Soon he is back in Paris studying new techniques of taking pictures and developing them. He was soon travelling in Europe and Russia, taking photographs and exhibiting them when he returned to London.

Fenton was so taken by photography that he called for the creation of a Photographic Society within Britain. He achieved his desire and was installed as its founder and first

Secretary. The organisation was to evolve over time into the Royal Photographic Society under the patronage of Prince Albert, the husband of Queen Victoria.

Plaque commemorating Roger Fenton

In the autumn of 1854 Fenton was approached by the government to go to the Crimea where a war was raging. It is believed that the reasoning behind this request was that certain newspapers – The Times has been cited in this - were not giving British forces a very good write-up. They thought that if Fenton could take photographs over there, they might help to show the British involvement in a better light. Fenton agreed to go and he spent approximately nine months in the war zone.

These days war photographers and film-makers are common sights in areas of conflict. New digital equipment is light and the technology can handle most of what may be thrown at it and produce good images. But things were very different for Fenton. His equipment was so bulky he had to have his own horse-drawn wagon to carry it all in. As a result he took his photographic assistant – Marcus Sparling – along with him.

Fenton also had another problem. Film was slow – meaning that long exposures were necessary to capture an image. This is fine for shooting a still-life in a studio but wars tend to have people rushing around and not posing for pictures in the heat of battle. So he was left with no choice but to pose some of his subjects artificially. In many ways the images still depicted the truth of what was going on but it was not "real" as we would expect today.

One of the most famous and badly judged incidents in military history took place during this war – it was what became known as the Charge of the Light Brigade. In essence, it amounted to a lightly armed brigade of cavalry men charging the massed guns of the enemy – the result was that they were cut to pieces. Fenton covered the landscape after the battle and he is believed to have photographed what became known as the Valley of Death. It was made famous by Alfred, Lord Tennyson in his poem.

Even though Fenton was in the Crimea as a civilian, he still suffered greatly for his art. The temperature during the summer months was uncomfortably high and he suffered a number of broken ribs after a fall. He also caught cholera but the scenes he witnessed also had a profound effect on him – he became depressed at the sight of so much death and suffering. But at the end of all this, he was able to produce 350 pictures covering the campaign. Upon returning to Britain 312 of them went on show both in London and around the country.

In the years following, Fenton travelled Britain taking pictures he considered works of art. But he was now up against a new breed of photographer – the equipment was becoming accessible to many and cheap portraits became the order of the day. Fenton fought hard against this lowering of standards as he saw it, but he was to lose out. The final straw came when the Royal Photographic Society demoted photography from being a pure art form to being a craft. This was too much for Fenton and in 1863 he sold all his equipment and went back into law as a barrister.

He was only fifty years old when he died at his home in Potter's Bar just north of London on the 8th August 1869. Although buried in the local church, his grave can no longer be seen as in 1869 the church was demolished.

Fenton's Regent's Park home

Humphrey Jennings

Address: 8 Regent's Park Terrace, London NW1

Station: Camden Town Tube

Humphrey Jennings was not a stills photographer but a documentary film-maker. He was born on the 19th August 1907 in Walberswick in Suffolk. Jennings certainly had creative genes as his father was an architect and his mother a painter. He read English at Cambridge University and graduated with a First Class Honours degree. At one time it looked as though he would follow an academic career but he soon left academia and tried a number of jobs including photography and theatre stage design. In 1929 he married Cicely Cooper and they had two daughters.

Jennings was a noted documentary film maker

It was in 1934 that he took his first step towards film-making when he joined perhaps the most famous documentary film unit of its time – the GPO Film Unit. The letters GPO stood for the General Post Office which over time evolved into the Crown Film Unit and then with offshoots, into the Post Office Film Unit and the British Telecom Film Unit. (I had the privilege of working for the latter as a cameraman, writer and director of film and video productions).

At first, Jennings did not sit easily within the unit but in 1936 he helped with the organisation of the London Surrealist Exhibition. He also became involved in the production of book titles based on the collected observations of various correspondents covering the coronation of King George VI and Queen Elizabeth. In addition Jennings produced a series of talks aimed at coal miners working in the Swansea Valley in south west Wales.

Jennings lived here from 1944-1950

When the Second World War broke out in 1939, the GPO Film Unit was within a year renamed as the Crown Film Unit whose main focus was to produce war propaganda for the Allies. It came under the control of the Ministry of Information. The output from this unit was considerable – consisting mainly of short documentary style films aimed at

161

informing and raising the morale of both the military forces and civilian population. Jennings was responsible for many of these but he also made one full length movie.

It was entitled "Fires Were Started." It is not the catchiest of titles and as a result the seventy minute long production was also known as "I was a Fireman." The purpose was to show and explain the work of the Auxiliary Fire Service in London during the war. Jennings used a number of new techniques including a montage of images on screen. For this the film is recognised as a classic of its type.

After the war he continued making documentary shorts including one for the Festival of Britain held in London in 1950. His film-making was in a way the cause of his death. He was on the Greek island of Porus scouting locations for a new film which was to cover different forms of healthcare in operation around Europe after the war. It is reported that he was at the top of some cliffs, slipped and fell to his death. He was buried in the capital of Greece – Athens.

Tony Ray-Jones

Address: 102 Gloucester Place, London W1

Station: Marble Arch Tube

Tony Ray-Jones was born on the 7th June 1941 in Wells in the county of Somerset. His father was a painter and etcher but when Tony was only eight months old, his father died. As a result, his mother moved the family to a number of different places before finally settling down in Hampstead in north London.

After he had finished his schooling, which apparently he hated, Tony attended the London College of Printing. His main area of study was graphic design. Still in his teens Tony took a trip to Africa where he took photographs. It is reported that a great many of them were taken out of his taxi window but the result earned him a scholarship to the Yale University of Art in the USA. He arrived at Yale when nineteen years old and within a couple of years he had proved his photographic ability by being hired by a number of prestigious magazines including The Saturday Evening Post and Car and Driver.

His studies brought him into contact with the renowned photographer Richard Avendon as well as a number of professional "street" photographers. Tony graduated from Yale in 1964 and then spent about a year travelling around the USA taking pictures and adding to his portfolio.

He moved back to Britain in 1965 and then spent the next five years living and working out of his studio in Gloucester Place. Although the 1960s was a time of celebrity and photographers were invited to all the best places, Tony felt that the serious role of commercial photography had not been recognised in this country. He set about to change this perception by producing a photographic book depicting the English at leisure. This was his personal project but he also had to earn a living which he did by producing portraits and executing photographic assignments for the Radio Times and other magazines.

His studio in Gloucester Place

In an interview conducted in 1968, Tony described what the foundations behind his desire for producing his book on the English at leisure. "My aim is to communicate something of the spirit and the mentality of the English, their habits and their way of life, the ironies that exist in the way they do things, partly through their traditions and partly through the nature of their environment and their mentality. For me there is something very special about the English 'way of life' and I wish to record it from my particular point of view before it becomes "Americanised" and disappears."

Over the years Tony produced a number of photo-journalistic collections for magazines which were well received. But he perhaps felt that his work was still not sufficiently recognised within his industry. He had tried unsuccessfully to be admitted to the prestigious Magnum Photos agency.

But he was still accepted by many to be a photographer of rare talent. So what was it that set him apart from many other photographers working at the time? Perhaps Sean

O'Hagen writing in The Guardian newspaper got it right when he wrote, "Ray-Jones was in many ways a social anthropologist with a camera, but it is his eye for detail and often brilliantly complex compositions that sets him apart. His images often appear cluttered ... On closer inspection, though, what we are glimpsing is several small narratives contained in the bigger defining one."

In January Tony returned to the USA and took up a teaching job at the San Francisco Art Institute and worked for both UK and USA clients in his spare time. But it was during this period that his health began to deterioate. He noticed that he was feeling exhausted and when he was tested the doctors' discovered he had leukemia. Tony travelled back to Britain and entered the Royal Marsden Hospital in central London for chemotherapy. Unfortunately his condition did not improve and he died on the 13th March 1972 just three days after arriving back in the country.

Plaque commemorating Tony Ray-Jones

Perhaps the best person to sum up his contribution to photography is Sean O'Hagen again. "In his short life he helped create a way of seeing that has shaped several generations of British photography."

Part Eight
Pilots

Douglas Bader

Address: 5 Petersham Mews, London SW7

Station: Gloucester Road Tube

Douglas Bader was an RAF pilot of whom it is fair to say was unique amongst his fellow aeronauts. A person of great inner strength and resolve he proved that a serious disability was no bar to achieving and exceeding any challenges presented to him.

Bader was born on the 21st February 1910 in London. He won a scholarship to attend St Edward's College in Oxford. From there he visited the Royal Air Force College at Cranwell. This was the spark that ignited his love for flying. He applied to Cranwell and was accepted as a pilot cadet in the RAF. He showed great promise both intellectually and as a natural sportsman.

In 1930 he achieved his initial aim and was awarded a commission in the RAF as a pilot. His first posting was to No 23 Squadron based at RAF Kenley. Bader soon showed that he had above average piloting skills and as such was selected to be one of the pilots in the squadron's aerobatic team. Unfortunately Bader was also a bit of a loose cannon and he would occasionally practice low level manoeuvres which had not been approved.

And it was whilst flying such a sortie at low level in December 1931 that he crashed. He was very seriously injured and this resulted in both of his legs being amputated. The doctors fitted him with two artificial tin legs. Within a short period Bader had not only learned to walk again on his new legs but he also discarded the walking stick that had been supplied. Bader had only one thing on his mind and that was to get back to flying.

He returned to the Central School of Flying and regained his pilot's licence. However the RAF had other ideas. To allow a pilot without legs back into a front-line squadron was unheard of. In fact there was nothing in regulations covering this situation. Instead they offered him a ground role which he refused. And so he resigned his commission, left the RAF and joined the Asiatic Petroleum Company.

Things may have stayed that way if the Second World War had not started. Immediately Bader was back asking that he be taken on as a pilot – after all there was a shortage of experienced pilots at that time. It worked and in June 1940 Bader found himself commanding No 242 Squadron. He found them to be in quite a state as they had taken many casualties in the recent Battle of France. But Bader, using his leadership qualities and high standards, turned the squadron around and they were soon ready to be fully operational again.

Bader was an RAF ace fighter pilot

During the summer of 1941 Bader showed how aggressive he could be in aerial warfare by claiming twenty two enemy aircraft – this was the fifth highest recorded by the RAF. Bader was promoted to Wing Commander and moved to head up a Wing at RAF Tangmere. However on the 9th August 1941 Bader was shot down over Le Touquet in northern France. He managed to bail out but both of his artificial legs were badly damaged.

The reason for the loss of his aircraft has been the subject of much debate. Bader believed he had collided with an enemy aircraft whilst Adolf Galland, the German air ace reported that his pilots' had shot him down. However, recent research seems to point to the situation being the result of friendly fire. But whatever the reason, Bader was captured by the Germans and made a prisoner of war.

He was taken to a local hospital where his legs were repaired. However the Germans did not count on the voracity of their patient. They became a little sloppy with his security and Bader being Bader made his escape with the help of the local resistance. Unfortunately he was eventually recaptured and taken to a new camp. But Bader was such a difficult prisoner to contain that he ended up in the maximum security prison of Colditz. It was said to be impossible to escape from. This didn't stop Bader from trying but he failed and remained there until his release by the Allies in 1945.

Bader's London home for twenty seven years

Upon returning to Britain he was promoted to Group Captain but he resigned from the RAF a year later. Bader re-joined his old company and rose to become managing director of one of their subsidiary operations – Shell Aircraft. He retired from there in 1969 and became a Board Member of the Civil Aviation Authority or CAA.

Bader still worked hard especially for the disabled and in 1973, he was awarded a knighthood for his efforts. He died on the 5th September 1982 in Chiswick, west London of a heart attack.

Geoffrey de Havilland

Address: 32 Baron's Court Road, London W14

Station: Baron's Court Tube

Geoffrey de Havilland was not only a pioneer of early aviation but he was also an aeronautical engineer responsible for the design of what is heralded as one of the best British war planes ever built – the Mosquito.

He was born on the 27th July 1882 in High Wycombe about twenty miles to the west of London. Like Douglas Bader, he was also a pupil at St Edward's School in Oxford. He graduated from the Crystal Palace School of Engineering. But his first work was in the field of automotive engineering, building cars and motorcycles. This was in fact the time that the Wright Brothers made their maiden flight in the first "proper" aircraft in the USA.

He married his first wife Louise in 1909 and at the same time embarked on his new career in aviation – building and flying aircraft. This was also the time that he lived in Baron's Court Road in west London. He borrowed money from his grandfather to start his company. It took two years to design and build his first plane and it had a pretty forgettable first flight – it crashed. A year later in 1910 he had the second one ready – a bi-plane which flew successfully.

Much bigger successes were to follow. In 1912 one of his planes established a new British altitude record of 10,500 feet. It was called the B.E. 2 and was on this occasion piloted by Geoffrey's brother Hereward. Today the Royal Aircraft Establishment at Farnborough is world-famous in aviation circles. But back in 1910 it was known as the HM Balloon Factory. Geoffrey joined the company and it was soon known as the Royal Aircraft Factory. Upon arriving Geoffrey sold the B.E. 2 to his employers and it became the first aircraft to have the Factory designation – it became known as the F.E. 1.

De Havilland's London home in 1910

In May 1914 he joined Airco in Hendon, north London where he was responsible for designing a number of planes. Each of them began with the title DH. Some of these are still flying such as the DH Rapide amongst others. This was also the time of the First World War and the newly formed Royal Flying Core or RFC used some of his designs at the front. The RFC would later become the Royal Air Force or RAF.

After the war Airco was taken over by BSA who were much more interested in manufacturing motor vehicles. So in 1920, Geoffrey raised £20,000 and bought out the aeronautical equipment of Airco and set up the de Havilland Aircraft Company. It was located at Stag Lane Aerodrome in Edgware to the north west of London. The output was large and included the Moth family of aircraft – some of which are still maintained in a flying condition today.

He was one of Britain's foremost aircraft designers

In 1933, the company moved to a new aerodrome at Hatfield in Hertfordshire. Geoffrey not only designed the planes but was also one of the test pilots. The output of new designs continued and when the Second World War broke out in 1939, they produced the Mosquito. Made of wood and metal it was fast and manoeuvrable – and loved by the pilots who flew it.

In 1944 they took over an aircraft engine company and formed the de Havilland Engine Company. This was to lead the company into designing jet aircraft. The first such engine was the Goblin gas turbine and it was incorporated into de Havilland's first jet – the Vampire. The company remained successful but in 1960 it was taken over by the Hawker Siddeley Company. He remained president of the company until his retirement in 1955. But he kept flying and did not stop until he reached the age of seventy.

He died on the 21st May 1965 of a cerebral haemorrhage. The de Havilland family had other aviators other than Geoffrey and his brother Hereward. Two of his three sons became test pilots but both were killed in aircraft accidents. These events were to cause his wife Louise to have a breakdown which led to her death. Geoffrey remarried in 1951 to Joan Firth and they remained together until his death.

Guy Gibson

Address: 32 Aberdeen Place, London NW8

Station: Warwick Avenue Tube

Guy Gibson was an RAF pilot who will always be remembered and associated with one bombing raid carried out during the Second World War. It was known as the Dambusters raid – a brilliantly conceived attack on the enemy's industrial ability - and he was the commanding officer.

He was born on the 12th August 1918, not in Britain but at Simla in India. This was because his father was a civil servant working overseas. Gibson did not remain in India for long for by the age of six he was back in England. It is said that it may have been a teacher who first introduced him to flying as he owned a World War I bi-plane. But whatever the reason, Gibson applied to join the RAF – and was rejected on the grounds that he was too small.

Not to be put off he reapplied when he was eighteen and this time was successful. He was awarded his commission on the 31st January 1937 and was posted to his first squadron – No 83 based at RAF Scampton. Originally the squadron was equipped with Hawker Hind light bombers but within two years they had the newer Handley Page Hampdens. On the first day of war being declared Gibson was tasked to fly out into the North Sea in order to bomb the German fleet. Unfortunately it could not be located and they returned to base.

It was some months before his squadron was called back into action. However, by the time his tour of duty had come to an end, he had been awarded the Distinguished Flying Cross. His next posting was as a flying instructor but this did not last long and he was soon back in action attached to No 29 Squadron. They were equipped with Bristol Beaufighters and based at RAF Digby. This tour saw him fly ninety nine missions and he was able to claim three kills. For this he was given a bar to add to his DFC. Gibson was also promoted to Squadron Leader.

Guy Gibson's London home

Because he had served two full tours Gibson was under no obligation to continue to be a front line pilot. However after a short spell instructing again he agreed to be posted to No 106 Squadron at RAF Coningsby. He was now flying the legendary Avro Lancaster four-engine heavy bomber. He now flew another twenty sorties bringing his total to 170. He was promoted to Wing Commander and received a further award, that of the Distinguished Service Order or DSO. Gibson was still only twenty four years old.

Both his personal qualities and his experience on Lancasters made him the perfect choice for a very special and secret mission. "Bomber" Harris the head of Bomber Command reckoned he was the right man for the job and so Gibson found himself in command of No 617 Squadron equipped with Lancasters.

The mission was to destroy a number of dams along the Ruhr in Germany. The resulting floods would put the industrial heart of Germany out of service. It would require a low-level attack at night and it would require a new type of bomb to do the job. It became known as the "Bouncing Bomb." There was one other complication – the squadron had less than two months to train and get the job done.

The inventor and engineer Barnes Wallis had designed the bomb and tests were carried out and the attack rehearsed at lakes around the country. The method of attack was a new one – it involved releasing the bomb at a certain height, speed and distance from the target. When the cylindrical shaped device hit the water it would literally bounce along the surface until it hit the dam wall in precisely the right point to breach it.

In all there were three dams targeted – the Mohne, the Eder and the Sorpe. The mission was heralded as a success after two of the dams were breached. However, many of the aircraft involved and their crews were lost on the mission. Gibson returned as a hero and was awarded the highest honour – the Victoria Cross. He became the most decorated pilot in the RAF.

Gibson was such a national hero that the powers-to-be did not want him to fly operationally again for fear of him being killed or taken prisoner. It would not be good for the general morale of the country if this happened. However Gibson had other ideas and he managed to convince the RAF to let him lead a massive bombing raid deep into Germany. They relented and on the 19th September 1944 he led the raid flying a Mosquito.

The raid was a success but later on Gibson's aircraft was seen to violently crash into the ground near Steenbergen in Holland. His remains were later recovered. The cause of the crash is still unknown.

It can be difficult to sum up a man like Gibson but perhaps the best attempt we have comes from Barnes Wallis himself. "For some men of great courage and adventure, inactivity was a slow death. Would a man like Gibson ever have adjusted back to peacetime life? One can imagine it would have been a somewhat empty existence after all he had been through. Facing death had become his drug. He had seen countless friends and comrades perish in the great crusade. Perhaps something in him even welcomed the inevitability he had always felt that before the war ended he would join them in their Bomber Command Valhalla. He had pushed his luck beyond all limits and he knew it. But that was the kind of man he was…a man of great courage, inspiration and leadership. A man born for war…but born to fall in war."

Gibson was a war hero to many

Amy Johnson

Address: Vernon Court, Hendon Way, London NW2

Station: Finchley Road Tube

Amy Johnson was one of Britain's best known female pilots. Her exploits were the stuff of adventure and she achieved a number of aviation "firsts" in her life. She was born in Hull in Yorkshire on the 1st July 1903. She gained a degree in Economics at Sheffield University in 1923.

She next moved down to London to find employment. Her first job was as a secretary in a law firm. This is apparently where she became interested in flying and she joined the London Aeroplane Club in 1928. This was a time when men dominated most activities and flying was no exception. However, Amy had other ideas. Not only did she learn to fly but at the same time she qualified as a trained aeronautical ground engineer. It has been reported that she was the first woman in the world to achieve this.

Amy Johnson was one of Britain's foremost aviators

This combination might have been enough for many but for Amy it was only just the start. She had much more daring ideas – in fact she set her ambition on flying to Australia – solo. It had already been achieved by a man – Bert Hinkler – in a time of sixteen days. Amy intended not only to copy his journey but to beat his record.

Raising money for the enterprise proved difficult at first but her father stepped in and paid half of the £600 asking price for a suitable aircraft – a DH Gypsy Moth registration G-AAAH. She named the aircraft "Jason" apparently after the family business trademark. Her epic flight began from Croydon Airport in south London on the 5th May 1930. Although she didn't beat the record she was the first woman to fly to Australia solo. She touched down at Darwin Airport on the 24th May 1930 after a flight of 11,000 miles.

On her return to Britain she was awarded a CBE. Did she now consider settling down? Anything but, as she now set her sights on flying from the UK to Japan in a Puss Moth. With her co-pilot – Jack Humphreys – they not only made it but set a new record. A year after this in 1932 Amy flew solo from England to Cape Town in South Africa.

In the same year she got married to Jim Mollison who was also a pilot. They made a team both in marriage and in the cockpit. Together they flew from South Wales to the USA non-stop in a DH Dragon. In 1934 they both competed in the London to Australia Air Race. The first stage to India they flew non-stop - setting a new record. Two years later she flew solo from England to Cape Town to recapture her record which she had lost.

In 1938 she and Jim were divorced. But soon there were other thoughts on her mind. The Second World War was about to begin and Amy wanted to be a part of it flying planes. As it was not permitted for a woman to be a front line military pilot she settled for the next best thing – ferrying an assortment of aircraft around the country for the RAF. The Air Transport Auxiliary needed experienced pilots and Amy had this in spades.

Unfortunately Amy would achieve another first – she became the first person in the Air Transport Auxiliary to be killed on active service. Mystery has always surrounded the circumstances around the crash. On the 5th January 1941 she was on a routine sortie to deliver an aircraft when she appears to have been shot down over the Thames Estuary. Her body was never recovered. So who shot her down?

Amy Johnson's London home

In 1999 a man by the name of Tom Mitchell claimed he was the person responsible. In a newspaper report which I read he says that her plane was shot down due to the fact that she did not give the code word which indicated she was a friend and not an enemy. These codes were changed daily and according to Mitchell they were left with no alternative when there was no reply to their requests. To this day we cannot be certain if this version of events is the definitive answer to the mystery and we may never know the truth. Some people believe there has been some sort of government cover-up but who knows?

On the 14th January a memorial service was held for her at St Martins-in-the-Fields in Trafalgar Square. Amy Johnson held a number of prestigious positions during her life.

And on a personal note, she was also the president of my own flying club back in the 1930s.

Amy Johnson about 1930

Thomas Sopwith

Address: 46 Green Street, London W1

Station: Marble Arch Tube

Thomas Sopwith was a British pioneer aviator and aircraft designer. However, he didn't spend all his time in the air as he was also an experienced America's Cup yachtsman, international ice hockey player, motor cycle racer and hot air balloonist. To fit all this in you need a long life and Sopwith achieved this as well by living to the ripe old age of 101 years.

He was born on the 18th January 1888 in Kensington, west London. But tragedy was to strike when he was ten years old. The family were on a holiday near Oban in Scotland. Thomas was sitting in a motor vehicle holding a loaded shotgun whilst his father drove. For some reason the gun went off and killed his father. The memory of this incident would haunt him all of his life.

By the time that flying took hold of him in 1910, Sopwith had already been an international hockey player, had been ballooning, taken part in motor cycle racing and started an automobile dealership in central London. However it was to be flying that would be the focus of his life. He was witness to the first commercial cross-channel flight. From that point, he made his first flight at Brooklands Aerodrome under the control of John Moisant. But learning to fly with a qualified pilot did not seem to fit in with Sopwith.

It is said that he taught himself to fly and on his first solo flight in a Howard Wright Avis monoplane, he managed to get neatly 300 metres before crashing. Not to be put off with such a trifling incident he soon took to the air again and this time was more successful. His crash was on the 22nd October 1910 and exactly one month later he was awarded his Aviation Certificate Number 31.

That's pretty good going by any standard. But he wasn't finished there – only three weeks later he had won a flying prize of £4,000 for making the longest flight from Britain to the Continent. In just under four hours he flew 169 miles. With the prize money he set up his own flying school at Brooklands.

Sopwith's home in Mayfair

Sopwith soon moved on to starting another company – Sopwith Aviation Company – which designed and built aircraft. They first rebuilt a Wright Model B plane and fitted a new engine to it. Then one of Sopwith's pilots – Harry Hawker – won the British Michelin Endurance prize for staying aloft for eight hours and twenty three minutes. This was quite an achievement for 1912 and soon the military were interested in purchasing some of his designs. The company moved to new premises in Kingston-upon-Thames.

With the outbreak of World War I in 1914, the military needed aircraft first for reconnaissance and then for fighting. Sopwith's company came up with the Sopwith Camel fighter and they sold over 18,000 of them. For his contribution to the war effort Sopwith was awarded a CBE in 1918. However the end of the war also brought financial problems to the company and it folded.

But from the ashes of the old emerged a new enterprise named after his chief engineer and test pilot of endurance fame – Harry Hawker. It was called Hawker Aircraft – one of the now legendary names from British aviation history. It evolved into the equally famous Hawker Siddeley Company and Sopwith remained with them even after it was nationalised. He stayed on as a consultant until 1980.

From 1934 to 1940 he lived at 46 Green Street Mayfair but in later life he moved to Hampshire with his wife Phyllis. On his 100th birthday he was able to witness a military flypast over his home. He died on the 27th January 1989.

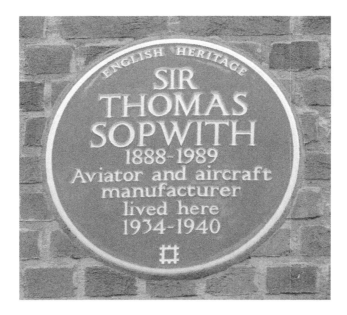

Sopwith had a long and varied life

Part Nine

Scientists

Charles Babbage

Address: 1A Dorset Street, London W1

Station: Baker Street Tube

In today's world computers are everywhere and it is true to say that western society would probably fall into chaos if they were removed. We've just become so used to them in our everyday lives that many members of the younger generation could not envisage life without them. But computers had to have been thought of as a concept first and the person credited with being the "father of the computer" is the British mathematician Charles Babbage.

He was born on the 26th December 1791. We believe his place of birth was at 44 Crosby Row, on the Walworth Road in London. However there has always been some dispute over this, so we cannot be absolutely sure if this is correct. His father was a successful banker and worked in Fleet Street. After attending various schools, Babbage went to Trinity College Cambridge to study mathematics. It is said he was unimpressed by the standard of teaching there and two years later he transferred to Peterhouse College, Cambridge where he received his degree.

His reputation as an exceptional mathematician soon found him lecturing at the Royal Institution on the subject of calculus. Within a couple of years he had been accepted as a member of the prestigious Royal Society. In 1820 Babbage was also instrumental in setting up another noble institution – the Astronomical Society.

Perhaps one of the most coveted positions in science is to be the Lucasian Professor of Mathematics at Cambridge University. It is a position that was once held by Isaac Newton and in recent years by Stephen Hawking. Babbage held this post from 1828 to 1839. This was also the time when he began devising a machine that could perform mathematical calculations.

He named it the "Difference Engine." It was a mechanical device and the first version used a combination of six wheels to make the calculations. It was successfully demonstrated to a number of audiences. But this was just the start. His "Difference Engine No 2" was to be bigger and more complicated. However he was also working on another device for making calculations. This one was called the "Analytical Engine" and it was a big step forward from his previous attempts.

The design of this new device would incorporate systems which are still recognisable today such as inputting data and instructions on punched cards. I remember these types of computers just a few decades ago. It was also designed to have a memory where numbers could be stored. Once again this was cutting-edge technology for the nineteenth century.

Unfortunately Babbage did not live long enough to see either his "Difference Engine No 2" or his "Analytical Engine" be completed. This was left to another brilliant British mathematician Ada Lovelace.

Site where Babbage spent the last 40 years of his life

On the personal side, he married Georgiana Whitmore on the 25th July and they had eight children. For the last forty years of his life they lived at 1A Dorset Street, Mayfair and it was here that he died on the 18th October 1871. His body underwent a post-mortem and from this we have a strange little tale. Babbage's brain was removed and cut in half. One side went to the Hunterian Museum in Lincoln's Inn Fields in London and the other half is on display at the Science Museum also in London.

Babbage was a pioneer of modern computing

Francis Crick

Address: 56 St George's Square, London SW1

Station: Pimlico Tube

Together with James Watson, Francis Crick was to make one of the greatest discoveries in biology. Their work was to earn them the Nobel Prize for medicine in 1962. Crick was born on the 8th June 1916 in Northampton. The Second World War interrupted his education and he was recruited to help develop magnetic mines which could be used by the Royal Navy to destroy enemy ships.

Crick's London home 1945 - 1947

When the war ended he was able to return to his main area of interest – science and in particular biophysics. By 1947 he was working at the Strangeways Research Laboratory at Cambridge University. Two years later he moved to Cambridge's Medical Research Council Unit located within the world-famous Cavendish Laboratories.

During this period Crick worked on determining the structure of large molecules within biological organisms. So when a biologist by the name of James Watson arrived from the USA in order to study the structure of nucleic acids, Crick was someone he wanted to talk to.

These acids were interesting and one in particular – deoxyribonucleic acid, better known as DNA, was even more so. It was believed that it played an important part in the hereditary determination of each cells' structure and function. Watson believed that if they could construct a three-dimensional model of DNA, then its role in hereditary processes would become clear. This fitted in well with Crick's own expertise.

Memorial to an exceptional scientist

They were eventually successful and a large part of the world came to know of DNA's structure – the double helix. But to get to this point was no easy matter. They utilised X-ray diffraction photography to help them begin to build the model. However, this was not enough as they then had to add DNA's physical and chemical properties into the mix.

Their work eventually led to scientists being able to understand gene replication and the nature of chromosomes. Finally they discovered that the DNA molecule can be read as a code which led to an understanding of the nature of cells.

In 1977 Crick moved to San Diego and worked at the Salk Institute for Biological Studies and held the role of professor there. He began work on the extremely difficult subject of the nature of consciousness which is still not fully understood. And it was in San Diego that Francis Crick died on the 28th July 2004.

Michael Faraday

Address: 48 Blandford Street, London W1

Station: Marble Arch Tube

Michael Faraday is considered to be one of the greatest scientists of all time. He was important in both the fields of physics and chemistry. His successes included the concept of the electromagnetic field, electromagnetic induction and the laws of electrolysis. But perhaps even more important in practical terms was that he was responsible for laying down the foundations of the electric motor and where would we be without that.

Michael Faraday – Man of Science

In chemistry he discovered benzene and also popularised many scientific terms including anode, cathode, electrode and ion. But if some of these words appear a little alien then he was also the inventor of an early version of something that every child will know about in a school laboratory – the Bunsen burner.

Faraday was born in Southwark, south London on the 22nd September 1791. His family were not well-off and Faraday received little in the way of a formal education. But he loved reading and this was the key to him gaining so much knowledge. He especially became interested in science and in particular electricity. Faraday had one advantage when it came to finding books to read – for seven years he was apprenticed to a bookbinder and seller. At work he could enjoy many of the books available at the time.

Faraday was an apprentice here

Through an association with the chemist Humphrey Davy, Faraday became Chemical Assistant at the Royal Institution. This was the start of what would turn out to be a long association with the Royal Institution. He became a member of the Royal Society in 1824 and a year later became the Director of Laboratory at the Royal Institution. He wasn't finished with this as six years later in 1833 he was appointed the first Fullerian Professor of Chemistry there. In 1826 he began the Friday Night Discourses and later the same year inaugurated the Royal Institution Christmas Lectures. These still exist today and the latter talks are broadcast by the BBC.

Faraday's contribution to science places him up there with the best. His early work on electromagnetic rotation would eventually lead to the electric motor. In 1831 he discovered electromagnetic induction which opened the world up to generators and transformers. Many of the words used by scientists and lay people were originally coined by Faraday. These as stated before included the terms "ion," "cathode" and "electrode."

Such was the esteem that Faraday was held in meant that he was awarded other official positions including Professor of Chemistry at the Royal Military Academy in Woolwich, south east London and the science advisor to Trinity House which was responsible for all lighthouses and lightships around the coast. He was also offered a knighthood which he turned down on the grounds of religion and stated that he always preferred to be known as plain Mr Faraday. The awards he did accept didn't only come from his own country. The science institutions from the Netherlands, Sweden and France all bestowed honours and membership of their societies.

But from the point of view of his health, all was not well. In 1839 he suffered a nervous breakdown and from the 1840s his health began to slowly deteriorate. He was given a grace and favour house in Hampton Court where he spent the rest of his life. And his life ended there – now 37 Hampton Court Road – on the 25th August 1867 aged 75 years. He is buried in Highgate Cemetery in north London after turning down an earlier offer of Westminster Abbey. However, there is a plaque to his memory there in the Abbey close to one of the other greats of science - Sir Isaac Newton.

Isaac Newton

Address: 87 Jermyn Street, London SW1

Station: Piccadilly Circus Tube

Isaac Newton was a mathematician and physicist who is regarded as one of the giants of science. His breadth of knowledge also stretched into chemistry and the early history of Western civilisation. And being referred to as a giant of science would have pleased him for it is said he had a high regard for his own talents and could be quick to anger if he received criticism.

He was born on the 25th December 1642 in Woolsthorpe in Lincolnshire. His early schooling was in Lincolnshire but in 1161 he enrolled to study at Cambridge University. He was awarded a degree and in 1667 he was made a Fellow of Trinity College. Two years later he became Lucasian Professor of Mathematics. This is a very prominent position and in recent years was held by Stephen Hawking. Over these years, besides lecturing, he was also working on a book which would become one of the foundations of science. It was called Principia, although its full title in English was Mathematical Principles of Natural Philosophy and was published in 1687.

But there was more to Newton than just science, much more. In 1689 he was elected as a Member of Parliament representing Cambridge University. This was mainly in order to oppose the King, James II's plan to change universities into Catholic institutions. In 1696 he became Warden of the Royal Mint which meant that he moved down to live in London. Three years later Newton was made Master of the Mint and he retained this position until his death. In 1702 he was back as a Member of Parliament.

Another great institution is the Royal Society and Newton became a member in 1671. In 1703 he became its president. This role lasts for one year and there is an election held to either re-appoint the current holder or appoint a new person to the position. Newton remained president of the society until his death, being re-elected each year. His work was recognised publicly in 1705 when he became a Knight of the Realm.

Newton lived here in Jermyn Street

Although it is said he had a high regard for his own talents, he was not a gregarious man, preferring instead to live life simply. He never married and so perhaps was able to apply himself to his work completely. By the end of the second decade of the eighteenth century Newton was acknowledged as the leading natural philosopher not only in England but in the whole of Europe. He was a foremost researcher in many branches of the physical sciences including optics, mathematics, mechanical engineering, gravity and chemistry.

There is story concerning Newton's "discovery" of gravity as a fundamental force of nature. It is known to many who would profess to know nothing of science. The story goes that Newton was sitting under an apple tree when one of the fruits fell from the tree and struck him on the head whereby he realised the force which made the apple fall also controlled the Moon and planets. It's a nice story but what is true is that he did calculate the force which was needed to keep the Moon in orbit around the Earth.

Commemorating Newton in London

Many of Newton's Laws stood the test of time and became the accepted explanation for many types of phenomena. This is especially true of his three Laws of Motion which every child who has studied science will know. However, over recent decades, Einstein's Theory of Relativity and Quantum Physics have somewhat overtaken Newton. But it is fairly safe to say that Newton's Laws hold up pretty well when taken on a "big" scale. They only show wanting when investigating phenomena on a quantum scale.

In addition he was also responsible for building the first reflecting telescope – preferred by optical astronomers, both professional and amateur. He was the first to show how white light was composed of the spectrum of colours by using a prism to separate the different wavelengths out. Newton formulated the empirical Law of Cooling and spent time studying the speed of sound.

On 5th July 1687 Newton published a book which is still held as one of the foundations of scientific knowledge. As previously stated it was the Principia and it set out to describe many natural phenomena. Many of his theories and laws were brought together in this book and it held "true" for nearly 200 years.

He died on the 31st March 1727 in Kensington. He spent a number of years living in Mayfair at 87 Jermyn Street. He is buried in Westminster Abbey. The poet Alexander Pope wrote a famous epitaph to him, "Nature and nature's laws lay hid in night; God said "Let Newton be" and all was light."

Alan Turing

Address: 2 Warrington Crescent, London W9

Station: Warwick Avenue Tube

Alan Turing was a brilliant man of science who excelled at mathematics, computer science, biology and artificial intelligence. He was also a cryptanalyst whose exploits were to play a huge part in winning the Second World War - more about that later. But he was also a troubled individual and was treated harshly by the authorities of the time.

Building where Alan Turing was born

Turing was born on the 23rd June 1912 in Maida Vale just north of central London. His potential was spotted early on and he was sent to Sherborne School in Dorset. However some of his tutors considered his great ability at mathematics not quite in line with a public school education which concentrated on the classics. At the age of sixteen he read Einstein's theories of relativity and it is generally believed that he understood them which would have been quite a feat even today.

Turing moved on to study mathematics at King's College Cambridge where he was awarded a first class honours in the subject. It was also about this time that Turing was studying and researching the beginnings of computer science. He postulated a universal Turing machine which would be capable of making calculations – in fact he felt it should be able to compute anything that was calculable. The paper he published is still taught to students of computation today.

During the Second World War Turing made one of his greatest contributions. The Germans had a method of encoding their messages called Enigma. Turing was sent to Bletchley Park where the code-breaking team was assembled. This organisation would later become GCHQ. Turing was able to come up with the idea of a machine which could crack the Enigma code more efficiently than other methods. In particular it was the naval Enigma variation that was the most difficult and Turing and his team was able to crack it. The work was top secret – and some details are still classified after seventy years - but it did give the Allies an enormous advantage over the enemy.

During this time Turing worked with a lady by the name of Joan Clarke. She was also a talented mathematician and cryptanalyst and in 1941 they became engaged to be married. Unfortunately it was not to last as Turing had to admit to her that he was gay. She in turn seemed to take the news in her stride. Later in the war, Turing moved to work on secure speech methods in radio telecommunications at the Secret Service's Radio Security Service.

In the years after the war he worked at the National Physical Laboratory researching an Automatic Computing Engine known as ACE. Unfortunately Turing did not live long enough to see a full-working model of ACE in action. In the early 1950s he was attracted to artificial intelligence and he formulated what became known as the Turing test whereby a computer or human attempts to answer a set of questions. If the computer fools the questioner into believing they are dealing with a human then the machine wins. Forms of this test are still in use today.

Up to this point Turing's career was spectacular in many ways but also secret. However, this was to change dramatically in 1952. He met a young man in Manchester and began a relationship with him. A burglary occurred at Turing's home and his partner said that the perpetrator was known to him. Turing reported this to the police and an investigation was started. Unfortunately it also uncovered the relationship between the two men. And at this time in Britain homosexuality was a crime.

He was found guilty of gross indecency and was sentenced to probation on account he received hormonal treatment for his "condition". This lasted a year. The conviction also had another consequence – he had his security clearances removed. In addition it stopped him visiting the USA where he had done much research in the past. He was still allowed to visit Europe and to keep his academic postings.

Alan Turing died on the 8th June 1954. His housekeeper discovered his body and a post-mortem deduced he had died of cyanide poisoning. There was a half-eaten apple close to him. It was not forensically tested but the inquest found that he had committed suicide by eating the poisoned apple. His body was cremated on the 12th June 1954.

Turing did not get the recognition he deserved

There have been a number of other theories put forward over the years as to the cause of death. One of the most likely is that he accidently breathed in cyanide fumes from a gas set-up in another room. Evidence for this comes from the post-mortem for it says that the damage appears to have come from inhalation rather than swallowing. His mother was reported as saying she believed he inadvertently contaminated the apple with the poison. At the other end of the scale, some conspiracy theorists think that he was murdered by the authorities for some reason but there is no real evidence for this.

Part Ten
Sports Stars

Jack Beresford

Address: 19 Grove Park Gardens, London W4

Station: Chiswick Overground

In 1996 the British rower Steve Redgrave took part in his fourth Olympic Games and won his fifth medal. This was not only an amazing performance but it also finally overtook the previous record for a rower which had stood for sixty years. The holder of this record was Jack Beresford who appeared in five consecutive Olympic Games and won a total of five medals. Redgrave also won five medals but he beat Beresford's collection of three gold medals and two silver by winning four gold medals and one bronze.

Jack Beresford – one of Britain's greatest rowers

Beresford was born on the 1st January 1899 into a successful rowing family as his father Julius had won a silver medal at the 1912 Olympics. He also won a number of competitions at the annual Henley Regatta. In addition Beresford's brother Eric was also a successful rower. At school Beresford not only rowed for Bedford School but captained their rugby team as well.

Unfortunately during the First World War he was wounded in the leg which cut short any hopes he had for playing rugby. But he was able to further his ambitions in rowing and in particular sculling. It was in 1920 that Beresford began to attain notable success – first by winning the Diamond Challenge Sculls at Henley Royal Regatta and then by winning a silver medal in one of the closest and most exciting single sculls' finals ever seen. He then went on the same year to win the Wingfield Sculls – he was to win this event for the next seven years, a record.

Beresford lived here from 1903 - 1940

Over the coming years he was to add many more medals and titles to his name. But it was his record at the Olympics that has gone down in history. Following his gold medal at the 1924 Olympics in Paris - four years later he won silver at the Amsterdam event by rowing in the eights. 1932 saw another gold in the coxless fours held in Los Angeles. Berlin in Germany was next. Beresford won gold in the double sculls. This was also the Games where the black American athlete Jesse Owens won the sprint competition which resulted in Adolf Hitler shunning him. Beresford was able and ready for his sixth

Olympics to be held in 1940. Unfortunately the Second World War intervened and the Games had to be cancelled.

From 1903 to 1940 Beresford lived at the same address in London – 19 Grove Park Gardens in West London. After his competitive career came to an end Beresford was in much demand to help head up and organise events within his sport. In 1946 he was elected Steward of the Henley Royal Regatta. Two years later the Olympics were held in London and Beresford was on the organising committee. He received a number of honours including the Olympic Order of Merit. In 1970 he became the President of the Thames Rowing Club and he held this position until his death in 1977.

Dorothea Lambert Chambers

Address: 7 North Common Road, London W5

Station: Ealing Broadway Tube

For all those who love tennis and even those that do not, the names of Roger Federer, Raffa Nadal, Novak Djokovic and the current British No 1 Andy Murray will be known to most. On the ladies side, Serena Williams, Steffi Graff and from Britain, Virginia Wade will also be familiar. And if we go back over the years many other famous names come to light. However, one of them will be a mystery to many but she achieved what many of the stars of today can only dream about.

She won an Olympic Gold medal for tennis in 1908

Her name was Dorothea Lambert Chambers and she was born on the 3rd September 1878 in Ealing, north West London. Under her maiden name of Douglass, she made her singles debut at Wimbledon in 1900. She received a bye in the first round and then lost in the second to a player by the name of Louisa Martin. But she persevered and three years later she had won her first singles title.

On the 6th April 1907 she got married to Robert Lambert Chambers and from that point on adopted his surname. One of the most cherished honours to be awarded amongst tennis players other than a grand-slam title is a gold medal at the Olympics. Andy Murray won his in London in 2012 and in 2016 in Rio. Dorothea won hers only a year after her marriage in a straight sets victory over Dora Boothby. This had the effect of boosting her profile and in 1910 she wrote a training book for aspiring tennis players which not only concentrated on technique but also recommended the type of equipment to be used and choice of clothes to be worn. This was very different to the technical clothing of today.

Chambers lived here for twenty years

I mentioned the name of Steffi Graff earlier. She was a fairly recent German player of exceptional talent – winning many grand-slams. During the Wimbledon Championships of 1911, Dorothea once again met Dora Boothby on the court – this time in the final. Dorothea won not only in straight sets but in what is now called a double bagel. This means that the losing player did not win any games during the entire match – the result being 6-0, 6-0. Steffi Graff managed the same feat in the French grand-slam in 1988 when she beat Natalia Zvereva.

The longest match at Wimbledon was a few years ago featuring Isner and Mahut which stretched over three days. There is a plaque on that court in Wimbledon marking the event. However, Dorothea also had a marathon match at Wimbledon in 1919. It was the longest to date and lasted forty four games. It was against the famous and great French player Suzanne Lenglen. Although Dorothea had two match points she eventually lost 8-10, 6-4 and 7-9.

Singles is a very physical sport and from 1921 on Dorothea decided to concentrate on playing doubles. She also captained Britain's Wightman Cup team for two years from 1924. In 1925 at the age of forty six Dorothea played both singles and doubles and won both of her matches. But it was soon time to hang up her racquet as a professional player. She did this in 1927 and used her experience to become a professional tennis coach.

She died on the 7th January 1960 at her home in Kensington at the age of eighty one. In 1981, Dorothea was inducted into the International Tennis Hall of Fame.

Tom Cribb

Address: 36 Panton Street, London SW1

Station: Leicester Square Tube

Today boxing has a mixed press – there are many fans worldwide but there are also others who believe that it should be banned on account of its violence. However, it is a very old sport with a long history and the rules under which it is conducted today make it a lot safer than it used to be. In fact the boxer we are about to discuss came from a time where gloves were not worn and often there was no limit to the number of rounds.

Illustration of Tom Cribb

Tom Cribb was born on the 8th July 1781 in Bristol which is about 120 miles west of London. But at the age of thirteen he had moved to London where he soon became a coal porter in Wapping. By 1805 he had his first boxing match in Wood Green – now a part of North London. He won his bout and when a month later, he won his second match, Cribb decided to turn professional and was taken under the wing of the promoter Captain Robert Barclay.

He was successful in many of his fights and by 1810 he was the British champion. Later that same year he fought an American former slave by the name of Tom Molineaux. The fight lasted thirty five rounds but at the end Cribb emerged victorious – he had also become the World champion. In a number of ways the fight was controversial and included Molineaux being injured when the crowd decided to invade the ring. As I said before, boxing in those days was not very well controlled.

There was a rematch in 1811 and Cribb retained his world title. It is reported he even fought Molineaux's trainer who was also a competitor. At the age of thirty one Cribb retired from the ring and became a coal merchant. He also found time to train other boxers on a part-time basis. This was followed by another change in career when he took over the running of a public house – Union Arms – in Panton Street, near to Leicester Square.

Pub has been renamed Tom Cribb

There are a number of accounts that state Cribb was undefeated during his whole career which would have been pretty amazing. However, the truth is also a bit special. He only suffered one defeat and that was on the 20th July 1805 to George Nicholls. Cribb retired completely in 1839 and moved to Woolwich in south east London. And it was here that he died on the 11th May 1848 – he was aged sixty six. He was buried locally and his grave is marked with a stone lion resting one paw on an urn.

Tom Cribb – bare knuckle boxing champion

W.G. Grace

Address: Fairmount, Mottingham Lane, London SE9

Station: Mottingham Overground

Cricket is a game which attracts many fanatical supporters around the world. As for the rest of the planet – they have no idea what on earth is going on and how it is scored. Many of the formal test matches will carry on for up to five days and end in a draw. But some new forms of the game last just a few hours and end up with a result. Many would also say that these are also far more exciting to watch. So opinion is divided amongst the "old school" and the new blood. However, both sides might agree on one thing – that one of the greatest players of all time was W.G. Grace.

William Gilbert Grace was born on the 18th July 1848 in Bristol. He trained as a doctor but he will always be associated with the game of cricket. Known as a right-handed all-rounder, he was only seventeen years of age when he played his first premiere class match. Being an all-rounder meant that he could bat, bowl and field to a high level.

Because many readers are not from Britain, you will be glad to know I will not try to explain the rules or how the game is scored. But if we consider some of the statistics Grace was responsible for in his career, most people will realise that he was a very special player. During his time he represented twenty eight teams not including his appearances for England.

Regarding the total number of runs scored in first class matches it is estimated that he made in the order of 54,000 runs. These included 120 centuries and 250 fifties. He also played for a total of forty four seasons – so there was no retiring early from the game for him. In fact the number of games he participated in was 850. During one eight day period he scored 800 runs. This included a couple of triple hundreds.

One of cricket's greatest players

His bowling was no less impressive – on one occasion he dismissed the whole of the opposing team of ten wickets in one innings for a total run score against him of just forty nine. To give you an idea of how special this is – it is still a record which has not been bettered in first class matches.

He made his first entry into the international game in 1880 against Australia and made a very valuable contribution by scoring 152 runs in the first innings. It is reported that this was also the first century that England had scored against the Australians. However, it is true to say that his international career was not as sparkling as his domestic one. Although he made a run score of 170 in one innings, his overall figures were not that spectacular. When his time with England finished he had scored just under 1,100 runs in twenty two test matches.

But he didn't give up the game completely. He joined the London County Cricket Club and spent eight years playing for them. This part of his career did not mean he was unimpressive. Although he was now approaching his 60s, he was still scoring thousands of runs each season. His last appearance in a minor match was in 1914 just before his 66th birthday. A year later he suffered a heart attack and died at the Fairmount Residential Care Home in south east London.

Care home where WG Grace died

Graham Hill

Address: 32 Parkside, London NW7

Station: Mill Hill Broadway Overground

Graham Hill is one of the legends of Motor Racing. During his career he won the Le Mans 24 Hours, the Monaco Grand Prix, the Indianapolis 500 and the Formula 1 Drivers' World Championship. He was born on the 15th February 1929 in Hampstead, north London. After he had finished his education he worked for Smith's Instruments. He served in the Royal Navy before returning to Smith's.

It is funny to think that he didn't pass his driving test until he was twenty four years old. And his first car was not one of the expensive flashy racers he would eventually drive. In fact Hill described it as, "a wreck" and "a budding racing driver should own such a car, as it teaches delicacy, poise and anticipation, mostly the latter I think!"

One of Britain's greatest racing drivers

His first taste of motor racing came in 1954 when he spent 25 pence on a lap at Brands Hatch in a Cooper 500 Formula 3 car. From that point on he knew what he wanted to do. In order to get more experience and to be a part of racing he was able to get a job as an engineer with the motor racing team Lotus. From there it was a just a matter of convincing the management to let him try out the cockpit for a test drive. By 1958 he was making his first appearance at a Formula 1 event for Lotus – at no other than the Monaco Grand Prix. Unfortunately he wasn't able to finish the race due to mechanical failure but he had made it into the big time.

It was in 1960 that Hill left Lotus to join the BRM team and within two years he had become World Champion. In 1966 he won the Indianapolis 500 driving a Lola-Ford. The next year Hill returned to Lotus and in 1968 became the World Champion for the second time. It has been written that the Lotus car at this time was not as strong as some others and during the US Grand Prix of 1969 Hill crashed and broke both his legs. Such was his character that he sent a message back to his wife saying that he would not be able to dance for a couple of weeks.

Graham Hill's home for twelve years

Although Hill recovered he did not have as much success as he had seen before. He moved to a number of teams over the coming years and was able to score points in some of the races. There was one bright accomplishment to come – in 1972 he won the Le Mans 24 Hour, racing for the Matra-Simca Shell Team. He also set up his own racing team in 1973 called Embassy Hill.

On the personal side of his life Hill married in 1955. His wife Bette gave birth to two daughters and one son. He was Damon Hill who went on to become a Formula 1 Racing Champion in his own right. Besides rowing which was an early interest of his, Hill also loved flying and owned a twin-engine Piper Aztec aircraft which he used to fly between race circuits and home. On one such flight on the 29th November 1975 he was returning from the Paul Ricard circuit in France. He had five passengers on board with him. Conditions were not good as he approached Elstree Aerodrome to the north of London. It was night and the weather was foggy. The plane crashed on Arkley Golf Course and all those on board were killed. The air accident investigation revealed that he was not rated for those conditions at that time.

Further Information

For further information about the author, go to

www.johnpullenwriter.com

www.facebook.com/JohnPullenWriter

Twitter: @johnpullenwrite

Other Books by the same Author

Secret Bloody London

Secret Dead London

Secret Criminal London

Secret Lost London

Secret Curious London

Secret Murderous London

Secret Haunted London

Where They Lived in London Vol 1

Flying the Dream

Fiction

Dragon's Claw

Dark Angel

Rogue Knight

Time Warrior

All available through Amazon or Createspace

Search "John Pullen" on www.amazon.co.uk

Made in the USA
Las Vegas, NV
21 October 2023

79471001R00129